BLACK BELT.
P R E S E N T S

THE ULTIMATE GUIDE TO
STRIKING

THE ULTIMATE GUIDE TO

STRIKING

Compiled by Edward Pollard
and Jeannine Santiago

Edited by Raymond Horwitz, Edward Pollard,
Jeannine Santiago and Jon Thibault

Graphic Design by John Bodine

Front and Back Cover Photos by Rick Hustead

Cover Models: Randy Word and Ignacio A. Cordero Jr.

©2006 Black Belt Communications LLC
All Rights Reserved
Printed in the United States of America
Library of Congress Control Number: 2006927302
ISBN-10: 0-89750-154-3
ISBN-13: 978-0-89750-154-5

First Printing 2006

BLACK BELT BOOKS
A Division of **OHARA** Ⓤ **PUBLICATIONS, INC.**
World Leader in Martial Arts Publications

FOREWORD

Drawing from more than a decade's worth of *Black Belt* issues, the editors have compiled *The Ultimate Guide to Striking* to present you, the reader, with virtually everything you need to know about the subject.

Written in various styles by a diverse group of contributors, *The Ultimate Guide to Striking* includes articles that appeared in *Black Belt* between 1990 and 2005. This unique book provides advice, techniques, scientific principles and philosophical theories on the subject of using one's arms and hands as weapons, written by world-class martial artists who practice everything from *shotokan*, *kenpo* and *shorin-ryu* karate to *jeet kune do*, *hsing-i-chuan*, American boxing and *jujutsu*. The varied topics covered include *wing chun's* elbow strikes, utilizing and countering a jab, and the little-known but brutal hand techniques of *kajukenbo*.

These entertaining and sometimes controversial essays will benefit all martial artists. Different eras and traditions are covered, from the archaic to the modern. The idealistic diversity and international flavor of the material will inspire the reader to gain greater insight into his own art while developing a greater appreciation for the contributions and theories of many others.

Although the martial arts are in a state of constant flux and innovation, we at *Black Belt* believe that, at this point in the vast history of the *budo*, this book is a representative sample of the striking techniques taught by the martial arts experts of the world.

CONTENTS

WING CHUN ELBOW STRIKES
Kung Fu With a Pointed Message

by Jane Hallander • Photos by Leung Ting • May 1990

Although the Chinese art of *wing chun* (also called *wing tsun* or *ving tsun*) is effective for both long- and short-range fighting, wing chun stylists prefer to get close enough to their opponents to use short-range punches and kicks that stick to and flow with the opponents' movements, destroying their defenses and creating openings. In addition to these techniques, however, wing chun features devastating elbow and forearm strikes.

Elbow and forearm strikes are among the mainstays of the wing chun system of Leung Ting, founder of the International Wing Tsun Martial Arts Association and a private student of the late Yip Man, the kung fu master who taught Bruce Lee the secrets of wing chun. Through his research into the style, Leung discovered that wing chun has many different origins. For instance, Yip's system contains branches in Fut Shan, China, which teach techniques different from those taught at Hong Kong schools.

Leung's research into wing chun's roots revealed that the original system went through many twists and turns during its development. Although Yip's wing chun branch has always been considered the most complete of its time, Leung's research indicates that many of the old instructors in Fut Shan, who were influenced by Yip, still retained their own unique teaching ideas.

Unfortunately, only bits and pieces of long-lost techniques survived, scattered and fragmented as the original wing chun system branched out. Leung claims to have pieced many of these fragments together and incorporated them into his own wing chun system. Included are seven interesting elbow techniques not seen in most Hong Kong wing chun schools.

Included in wing chun lore is its suspected role in the creation of the Thai art *ling lum* (flying monkey), which uses many elbow and knee techniques that closely resemble present-day wing chun. Wing chun's influence may also have extended into the art of *muay Thai*, which was said to have its roots, especially its devastating elbow and knee strikes, in ling lum.

The elbow has a sharp, pointed structure, making it the body's most dangerous natural weapon. A person who knows how to use elbow strikes can administer a penetrating blow to a small area of the opponent's body. Because the force to a small area is greatly concentrated, it causes much more damage than the widely dispersed power of a regular fist or palm strike. Of course, because they are potentially damaging, elbows should be used only when other, less-dangerous techniques have not finished the opponent. If timed right, elbow techniques are good for both defense and attack.

So when is the right time for a wing chun elbow strike?

Leung says you should be very close to your opponent before you use your elbow. An elbow technique has the reach of half an arm length. When the distance between you and your opponent is more than that, use another technique.

For instance, if the distance between you and your opponent is two feet, all you need to do is straighten your arm and deliver a punch, which does not change the distance between you and the opponent. However, if you use an elbow technique at the same distance, you must move your body much closer to the opponent before your elbow can strike him. While you are moving closer, the opponent has time to attack before your elbow even reaches him.

Leung Ting (right) demonstrates *wing chun's* vertical elbow strike known as *chik lok jarn*. He faces off (1) with an opponent who rushes forward (2) and grabs Leung's waist, making it difficult for the latter to use a punching technique. Instead, Leung uses his left palm to press (3) his opponent's head down, then delivers (4) a vertical elbow strike to the spine.

Wing chun expert Leung Ting demonstrates the back elbow strike known as *hau jarn*. Leung is attacked (1) from behind, but he raises (2) his right arm and twists his body to the side, creating room for an elbow strike.

"If given a choice, always strike with your fist or palm rather than your elbow," Leung says. "When you attack with a fist or palm, your entire arm moves. The parts of your body closest to your opponent are the fist and forearm. Normally, your opponent blocks your hand attack by stopping your forearm function. Even if this happens, you can still use an elbow technique with the uninhibited function of your upper arm. However, if you start with an elbow strike, that is also your last effort; you have nothing left if your opponent reacts well."

Let's assume you're involved in a serious self-defense situation where you have no choice but to use an elbow strike. Your assailant is determined to injure you, and you're within half an arm's distance of your attacker. Which of the seven wing chun elbow techniques should you use?

Yip's Hong Kong students learned only one elbow strike, and his Fut Shan students knew three elbow techniques. Leung's wing chun system uses the three original techniques—*kup jarn*, an overhead elbow strike; *kwai jarn*, a kneeling or diagonal elbow technique; and *pai jarn*, a horizontal hacking elbow strike—as well as four others.

Kup jarn is a high elbow strike that drops down on its target, usually the opponent's head.

Kwai jarn is a diagonal, curving elbow attack that rakes down the opponent's centerline, starting with the face. Unlike other elbow strikes, kwai jarn doesn't use the point of the elbow for a single, direct blow to the

Leung simultaneously grabs (3) his opponent's right arm and pulls him (4) into an elbow strike to the ribs.

body. Instead, the kwai jarn technique slices down the opponent's body like a knife. Targets include the opponent's temple, face, neck, collarbone and chest. It's a very effective technique for escaping and countering a front choke hold.

Pai jarn is an elbow chop delivered horizontally to the assailant's face. This technique works well as a counter to a bear hug, where you have little room to maneuver. It can be delivered with both arms as a double elbow strike, or with a single arm.

Pai jarn is delivered by first bending the forearm at right angles to the upper arm. A sharp twist of the waist brings the elbow into striking range. If the target is the side of the opponent's head, Leung likes to hold the assailant's head with the other hand, which keeps him from moving his head away from the sideways elbow strike.

Wing chun's *chum kil* form contains an elbow technique called *lan sau* (forearm strike). In this technique, the elbow is not the striking surface, but because the elbow is bent sharply, it is considered an elbow technique. As the wing chun practitioner turns his body, the forearm strikes the opponent's head, neck or chest with tremendous force. This technique draws most of its power from the torque created by the sharp turning of the body.

Ping jarn (horizontal sideward elbow), which is found in the *sil lum tao* wing chun form, is an elbow strike delivered straight into the target

Leung Ting (right) demonstrates *wing chun's* horizontal elbow strike, known as *pai yarn*. Leung is grabbed (1) in a bear hug. He reaches up (2) with his right hand and pulls his opponent's head into a left horizontal elbow smash (3).

with the practitioner's arm in a horizontal position. This is a devastating elbow strike when used against soft, vulnerable parts of the body, such as the throat.

Hau jarn (back elbow strike) is a rear elbow strike seen in wing chun forms whenever the fist is drawn backward. Most wing chun stylists see the withdrawal of the fist as strictly a transitional action between two sets of movements. Actually, the elbow in this withdrawal action is a deadly attack, more powerful in fact than a fist. Like ping jarn, it is a straight elbow technique with the fist turned upward, aimed at an opponent directly behind the wing chun stylist. The striking area is the sharp point of the elbow. The seventh wing chun elbow technique in Leung's system is *chik lok jarn* (vertical elbow strike), a downward elbow strike used at very close range when there is no room for any other hand technique. Chik lok jarn might be used against an opponent who rushes headfirst toward the wing chun stylist, burying his head away from the defender's reach. This technique is usually directed at the top of the opponent's spine, striking with the point of the elbow.

Elbow techniques are the last resort in wing chun kung fu. However, "last resort" doesn't necessarily mean they are not among the system's most effective techniques. It simply indicates that when you are within the proper range and need a defense that may do your opponent great injury, you might want to consider wing chun elbow strikes.

THE JAB
Kickboxing's Most Neglected Technique

by Graciela Casillas • July 1990

The jab is one of the most effective punches in both boxing and kickboxing. A jab that connects with speed, power and accuracy can determine the outcome of a fight. This was evident in the recent Buster Douglas – Mike Tyson fight, when Douglas' ability to hit Tyson with the jab was a major factor in the challenger's upset victory.

The jab's effectiveness is often taken for granted, however. It is viewed as an elementary punch that takes little effort to cultivate. But like all combat techniques, it takes time and dedicated practice to perfect the jab. The first step is to isolate the jab and concentrate on mechanics. The following are some of the jab's basic elements:

• **Stance and guard**—To execute a left jab, stand with your left foot forward, bend your knees slightly and raise your right heel, stepping on the ball of your right foot. Both hands are held high. Hold your right fist against your cheek, and lead with your left hand. Those who are left-handed can simply reverse this position.

• **Elbow**—When initiating the jab, the punch moves in a straight trajectory with the elbow aligned with the fist for skeletal support. Jabbing with

Although the jab is often viewed as an elementary punch that takes little effort to cultivate, it is one of the most effective techniques in both boxing and kickboxing.

the elbow out not only results in a less-powerful punch, but the telegraphed movement makes it easy to counter.

• **Fist**—The fist extends in a vertical position and is supported by the elbow. Before striking the target, the fist is rotated to a horizontal position. When executed with speed, this movement creates the snap in the jab. The punch may not appear powerful, yet the twisting of the wrist and the speed of delivery creates a stunning effect.

• **Shoulder**—The shoulder follows the elbow. This is an area where many fighters tend to be weak. Not realizing that power comes from proper body mechanics, they attempt to wind up, telegraphing the jab. A skilled opponent can counterattack before the movement is completed. Concentrate on moving the fist first, allowing the elbow and shoulder to follow.

• **Footwork**—There are many ways to incorporate footwork with the jab. In the most basic method, you push off the ball of the rear foot as you advance. The momentum of the body moving forward, synchronized with body mechanics, increases the power of the jab. This concept applies whether you are moving forward, backward, angling or circling.

• **Retraction**—Keep the jabbing hand up after retracting it so it is in position to protect your head. Surprisingly, many fighters struggle with this apparently simple task.

The following are some basic combinations using the jab:

• **Jab and cross**—Often fighters do not follow up with the cross after hitting with the jab, thinking the opponent is out of range. The rule to remember is that, if you can make contact with the jab, you can make contact with the cross. It is my observation that the primary reason fighters miss with the cross is because of timing. They wait until they have retracted their jab before throwing the cross. The cross should pass the left hand as the jab is retracted.

Power can be added to the jab by placing your entire body behind it, stunning the opponent as you follow up with the cross. You can also set up the cross by using the jab to distract the opponent's vision.

• **Jab and hook**—Because the left hook is easily telegraphed, using the jab to set it up is very effective. Be careful not to overdue it, however. If you jab and hook with the lead hand, you may get away with it once or twice, but if your rhythm is predictable, your opponent will see the pattern and prepare a counter. The key is to deliberately establish a predictable rhythmic pattern in order to break it once your opponent reads it. My first knockout in the ring came via this concept. After establishing a predictable pattern, I faked with the jab, sidestepped and threw the left hook.

• **Jab and uppercut**—The uppercut is difficult to master, and most fighters tend to telegraph this technique by throwing it wide. The jab, however, can help camouflage the uppercut. Again, timing is essential. Depending on the style and attitude of the fighter, he can jab and immediately follow up with the uppercut, or he can throw multiple jabs until an opening for the uppercut is created.

• **Jab and kick**—Rear-leg kicks are usually telegraphed and easy to counter if not accompanied by another punch or kick. Use the jab to camouflage the kick. The rear-leg kick should be initiated before the jabbing hand returns to its resting position.

The jab is also effective in setting up lead-leg kicks, especially when your opponent consistently moves away. You can deliver the jab and, as the opponent pulls away, follow up with the lead leg.

Once you have jabbed and hit your opponent with the cross, hook or uppercut, your options are numerous. You may choose to follow up with punches or kicks to the body, or to move out. Continue to jab as you move away, and be sure to keep your guard up.

The jab can be a powerful and deceptive punch. It is versatile and can be used offensively or defensively. It can be used to set up your opponent for a knockout punch or kick, and it can be used to counterpunch. The jab should be thoroughly explored in training, for as Douglas learned, it can make a very big difference in the ring.

COUNTERING THE JAB

by Graciela Casillas • August 1990

In his recent boxing match against Buster Douglas, Mike Tyson learned that a well-placed jab can have a tremendous effect on the outcome of a fight. Developing a swift, powerful jab should be a priority for every fighter, whether he's a boxer or a martial artist. Then again, there is no such thing as a perfect technique, and the jab, like any other punch or kick, can be countered.

There are many countermeasures to the jab, each with its own advantages and disadvantages. Following are some of the basic defenses and counters for a jab that I used while competing in kickboxing and boxing:

• **Slip**—You slip a punch by moving your head quickly out of its trajectory. The most effective way to slip a jab is to move diagonally inside or outside. Beware of the opponent's cross when slipping inside of his guard. Once you slip the punch, recover to a ready position. The slip is a purely defensive maneuver against the jab.

Slipping develops reflexes and teaches a fighter not to flinch. The novice is likely to close his eyes or turn away when he sees a punch coming. Eventually, slipping becomes an instinctive reaction and the fighter develops the mental ability to stay focused under pressure.

> *When parrying, remember to keep your rear hand high, relaxed and ready to respond.*

• **Rear-hand parry**—Use the right hand to deflect the jab while the left leg is forward. This is a very fast counter and is one of the most common techniques taught by trainers. But although the parry appears to be a simple movement, mastering it requires speed, timing and accuracy. In order to parry effectively and consistently, the technique must be a short, economical movement. Overextension sets the fighter up for a double jab or a fake. When parrying, remember to keep your rear hand high, relaxed and ready to respond. Once you have parried the jab, return the rear hand to its ready position.

• **Front-hand parry**—The front hand can also be used to deflect a jab, but it is not generally encouraged because it removes your lead hand from a protecting position in front of your face. Unless you are highly skilled, there is a tendency to overextend the parry, which creates an opening

19

for your opponent's right cross. The front-hand parry thus puts you in a vulnerable position. Nevertheless, it is effective against kicks because you are out of hand range and have more time to react to your opponent's follow-up technique.

• **Slip and parry**—Once you feel comfortable with the slip and the parry separately, practice doing both simultaneously. Eventually, it becomes second nature to slip as you parry, and you will feel more secure using the two together. Using both techniques simultaneously guarantees that you will not be hit if you happen to exaggerate the parry and miss the punch with your hand.

• **Bob and weave**—This is one of the most misunderstood ring tactics. I always tell students that, unless they intend to counterattack, they are better off stepping back than attempting to bob and weave. It is an ideal strategy for the counterfighter. Bobbing and weaving beneath your opponent's cross places you in a position to follow up with a hook. Bobbing and weaving beneath his left hook puts you in position to throw your right cross. In essence, you evade his strike and punch in the process. The momentum created by your bob and weave adds power to the punch.

Developing a swift, powerful jab should be a priority for every fighter, whether he's a boxer or a martial artist.

If you bob and weave beneath a punch, be sure to keep your hands up and your knees bent. The most common mistake is to bend beyond your center of gravity and lower your head. This not only upsets your balance but also leaves you vulnerable to a knee strike or a kick.

There are many ways to defend against or counter a jab. Defense should be approached with an aggressive attitude. Whether you block, slip, parry or bob and weave, immediately follow up with a punch or kick of your own. If you are close enough to parry a punch, you are close enough to deliver a punch. Every move you make should have a purpose.

SHORIN-RYU OPEN-HAND TECHNIQUES
Self-Defense at Your Fingertips

by Phil Lusignan • Photos by Ashley Massey • December 1990

For someone proficient in Okinawan *shorin-ryu* karate, self-defense is as close as your fingertips.

One of the oldest of the traditional karate styles, shorin-ryu's strong Chinese influence is evident in its predominant use of hand techniques, especially those employing the fingers or open hand.

When danger arises on the street, the wise karateka will want to put an end to the confrontation as quickly as possible and effect his escape.

Shorin-ryu practitioners are known for their strong punching abilities, but the style has an equal reputation for the use of fast, snakelike fingertip strikes to the soft, vital points of the human body. Because of today's widespread use of foam-rubber sparring gloves that cover the knuckles and back of the hand, finger strikes and open-hand techniques are not as widely practiced as they once were. The obvious danger of injury to the opponent that goes with the use of these techniques makes them impractical (and illegal) for tournament competition. But for *karateka* concerned with self-defense, such techniques can be extremely effective.

When danger arises on the street, the wise karateka will want to put an end to the confrontation as quickly as possible and effect his escape. If an assailant cannot see or cannot breathe, he will likely have great difficulty continuing any type of attack. Shorin-ryu's rapid eye gouges and piercing spearhand thrusts to the throat can leave the assailant rolling on the ground, disoriented and gasping for breath, allowing the would-be victim an opportunity to escape. Shorin-ryu was developed specifically as a method of self-defense. Although the style's techniques were developed long ago, they may be as practical now as they ever were. With street violence on the rise, people are looking for effective methods of protecting themselves. In shorin-ryu, they may find just what they are looking for.

Because the art's hand techniques rely on speed and penetration, they can be delivered equally well by individuals of all sizes. Women find that they can use these techniques equally as well as men. With the additional element of surprise, the female shorin-ryu practitioner may find that she has the ability to defeat a much larger opponent.

Shorin-ryu students are by no means limited to the fingertips or knuckles when choosing hand techniques. The edge of the hand, the wrist, the palm and even the elbow can be called on to act as weapons of self-defense. Most of these techniques can be found in the art's *kata* (forms), the living textbooks of shorin-ryu.

The position of the fingers, as well as the rest of the hand, is very important when attempting to execute shorin-ryu hand techniques. An eye gouge, for example, is best performed with the fingers spread, allowing a better chance of hitting an opponent's eyes with one of the fingertips. It must be remembered that human targets are almost never stationary,

Shorin-ryu karate stylists learn to use the art's techniques in combinations. In the photo above, shorin-ryu instructor Cindy Lusignan combines an open-hand strike with a leg sweep to take down an assailant.

Some of *shorin-ryu* karate's open-hand techniques include eye gouges with the fingers (1) and inverted spearhands, called "cobra strikes" (2).

and the head, in particular, is usually moving when a strike is attempted toward it. The spread-finger position allows for some success even when the strike lands slightly off target.

Conversely, a spearhand thrust to the throat is implemented with the fingers pressed tightly together. The throat provides a wider but somewhat more solid target. This hand position provides a stronger striking surface that is more likely to inflict damage when it hits the target.

The knifehand and ridgehand strikes use the outside edges of the hand, just as their names imply. The hand is rigid at the point of contact for both of these techniques, which can be delivered to nearly any vital area of the body, but are most often targeted to soft spots such as the nose, throat and side of the neck. The palm-heel strike is another effective shorin-ryu open-hand technique. This strike can be used effectively against almost any body target, although the nose and the point of the chin are two of the most popular.

One of the more exotic shorin-ryu hand techniques is the "dragon's tail," also known as the bent-wrist strike. The striking surface is the point at which the wrist and the back of the hand connect. When striking, the hand is bent away from the target surface and the back of the wrist makes contact.

Spearhand thrusts (3) and "dragon's tail" (bent-wrist) strikes (4) are also effective.

This technique can be used effectively against almost any target area, but the most common are the nose, jaw, throat and back of the neck.

Another of the more unusual shorin-ryu hand techniques is the "cobra strike"—an inverted spearhand thrust with the palm turned up. The eyes and throat are the most common targets for this technique. It is especially

Shorin-ryu's open-hand techniques do not necessarily take the place of closed-fist punching.

effective after using a ridgehand to block a punch, whereby the "cobra" strikes the opponent's eye by slipping over his extended punching arm.

Elbow strikes are also commonly used in shorin-ryu and are found both in the kata and practical self-defense drills of this Okinawan style. The elbow can be thrown like a forearm strike to the rear to the side. It can also be used as an uppercut in close-quarter fighting.

Several shorin-ryu open-hand techniques can be used as blocks as well as strikes. Knifehands and ridgehands can be used for blocking or as a means of deflecting an opponent's blows. The palm-heel and dragon's-tail strikes can also be effective blocking maneuvers.

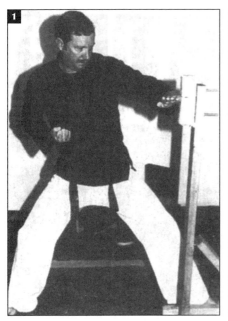 

Shorin-ryu stylists can practice their open-hand techniques on the traditional *makiwara* (1), striking dummy (2) or a heavy bag.

Learning to use shorin-ryu's open-hand techniques in combination with one another is very important. As previously mentioned, the cobra strike can be employed effectively in combination with the ridgehand block. A dragon's-tail block followed by a palm-heel strike is another effective combination of open-hand moves. And a palm-heel strike to the nose can be followed by an eye gouge with the same hand.

Knowing the location of the body's vital points, including the primary nerve centers, is very important when using open-hand strikes. The most obvious targets are the eyes, ears, nose and throat, but hitting a number of other delicate areas can also be extremely effective: the solar plexus, groin, kidneys, the carotid artery on each side of the neck, the nerves directly under the ears, and the ribs. There are also nerve centers on the inside of the upper arm and in the armpit that, when properly struck, can make an assailant think twice about launching a second strike.

Shorin-ryu training teaches a martial artist to strike quickly to a vital target in order to stun and disorient the assailant. This will usually stop the initial assault and allow the defender to counterattack, possibly with a strong, low, straight-line kick, which shorin-ryu is noted for. If the defender can blur the attacker's vision with his initial counterstrike, he should be able to escape.

Shorin-ryu's open-hand techniques do not necessarily take the place of closed-fist punching. In fact, they may even complement them or act as setup strikes. An excellent combination would be to blind an opponent with a left-hand eye gouge and follow immediately with a series of hard punches with the right hand. An open-hand strike can also lead to a grab

The female shorin-ryu practitioner may find that she has the ability to defeat a much larger opponent.

that would allow the defender to pull his opponent off-balance and deliver an effective follow-up technique. The hands can also be used for executing leg traps and takedowns. For instance, a ridgehand strike to the body can set up a hip throw or sweeping takedown.

There are a number of ways to perfect shorin-ryu open-hand techniques. Some of the harder strikes, such as the knifehand, ridgehand, palm-heel and bent-wrist techniques, can be practiced on the *makiwara* (punching board) or heavy bag. Techniques such as the eye gouge and spearhand thrust can be practiced on a speed bag, a tennis ball hanging from a rope, or even a rag or towel hanging from the ceiling. Push-ups on the fingers and the backs of the wrists also help strengthen these strikes.

Few, if any, of shorin-ryu's open-hand techniques will earn a tournament fighter any points in the ring. In fact, they would probably get the competitor disqualified. But in a street confrontation, the winner is the one who walks away unharmed. And shorin-ryu's open-hand techniques might be just the edge a karateka needs to get home safely.

KENPO KARATE'S REVERSE PUNCH
Sock It to Your Opponent

by Jane Hallander • Photos by Jane Hallander • January 1991

Probably the best-known and least-understood technique in *kenpo* karate is the reverse punch. Often considered a simple, basic technique, the reverse punch is actually a highly refined and efficient sparring and self-defense tool.

Kenpo instructor Estuardo "Stuart" Schumann of West Hills, California, has taken the reverse punch to a new dimension. Schumann is noted for his many kenpo schools in Guatemala, and each year he takes students to the Pan-American Nationals in Miami, where they have enjoyed great success, particularly by utilizing the reverse punch.

Besides basic reverse punches, Schumann teaches a special "freestyle" reverse punch. Developed for close-range fighting, this punch is not cocked back to the side like conventional reverse punches. Instead, it comes directly from the hip, re-chambering the punching arm simultaneously with the hip's recoil. The punching hand is kept toward the front, where it benefits from the relaxed snap of good hip rotation.

As the freestyle reverse punch is launched, the punching hand's wrist moves straight forward, locking into place at the same time the hip snaps forward. Schumann's secret is hip action that starts relaxed, snaps forward, then relaxes and finally recoils back to the starting position.

Because joints naturally bend in one direction only, Schumann aligns the wrist joint with the rest of the arm. Then, when impact with the target occurs, all forward punching motion comes in a straight line from the hip. Rotating or snapping the hip toward the target helps extend and straighten the punching arm and shoulder.

Regular reverse punches are accomplished by cocking the elbow back and lifting the arm to waist level. But with Schumann's freestyle reverse punch, the arm stays at hip level and the punch is faster and more direct.

Unlike conventional reverse punches, in which the body sinks as the fist extends, Schumann finds that it's much faster and just as accurate to simply turn the hips toward the target without lowering the body. The practitioner is still punching from a relatively low center of gravity—starting low and finishing low—but does not drop down during the technique.

The lower back connects the upper and lower body during a reverse punch. From a low center of gravity, the back doesn't absorb all of the punch's shock and recoil. Instead, it channels the shock down through the legs to the ground.

"We try to maintain kenpo stances with a low center of gravity. That helps make the punches more direct and fluid," Schumann says.

Lower-back connection and hip action are what give reverse punches their devastating power. The lower back connects the practitioner's legs with his upper body, drawing power into the upper torso. From that connection, the waist and hips direct power into the punching arm and fist. Without correct lower-back position and hip action, the reverse punch is merely a shoulder and arm exercise.

Estuardo Schumann demonstrates (1 and 2) a traditional *kenpo* reverse punch, executed from a square stance, with the elbow of the punching arm cocked back and held high. The technique is in sharp contrast to Schumann's freestyle kenpo reverse punch (1a and 2a), in which he assumes a boxing stance and the arm is not cocked.

Estuardo Schumann's students hone their reverse-punch skills by "circle training. " Schumann (right) demonstrates by squaring off (1) against a student in a small circle and feinting (2) a punch to the body,

"Our reverse punches are done with form and speed, not power," Schumann says. "Power comes naturally when you learn the correct body connection. With good form, you get a sharp, clean punch. Hip power gives you extra speed. The rest happens naturally."

Schumann's reverse-punch training techniques are based on a study of what works in real-life situations. Even the way he makes a fist illustrates his attention to important details.

"We *fold* the fingers into the palm, locking the fist with the thumb across the index and middle fingers," he explains. "If you just *close* your fingers, the fist is hollow and weakens the joints of the hand."

Schumann's students hone their reverse-punch skills by conducting what he calls "circle training," a punching method that combines mobility and angles of attack with the concept of not retreating from an opponent. Although students practice in an actual circle painted on the floor, the circle theory is really a concept, designed to keep the opponent busy warding off your blows and wondering where the next strike will come from. The idea is that you cannot be too direct with a reverse punch. If you are, you will telegraph the technique and your opponent will block it.

"Circle practice teaches students to 'talk' (feint) to their opponents with their hands. It gives their movements flow and rhythm. They no longer make stop-and-go punches," Schumann states. "They are quick and light on their feet as power flows naturally out through their fists."

Circle training resembles shadowboxing. Students learn to keep moving and distract imaginary opponents with their hands, always measuring the distance and looking for an opening. Students move in a perpetual circle, using various angles of attack. They also develop footwork similar to that

then delivering (3) a right to the head and (4) a left to the body.

used by boxers, allowing them to disrupt an opponent's timing. They learn to close the distance between themselves and their opponent by using only basic reverse-punch combinations, not fancy spinning or jumping techniques. Circle training, therefore, leads to practical fighting tactics.

Schumann has both large and small circles outlined on his school floor. He starts students in the large circle, gradually advancing to the smaller one. The large circle teaches them mobility, while the small one familiarizes them with close-range sparring.

After individual circle training, Schumann's students graduate to partner sparring. However, this isn't your everyday point sparring. The students actually hit each other, while concentrating on their form and speed. They wrap their hands and wear sparring gloves for protection.

Karate has evolved a lot since it first appeared in Japan, and the kenpo reverse punch is no different. Its evolution has made it more powerful and more dangerous. With proper training, the simple reverse punch can become the most effective technique in your fighting arsenal.

SPEED-BAG TRAINING
Add a Little Lightning to Your Fighting Techniques

by Alan Kahn • Photos by Ron Mahan • May 1991

The speed bag is an extremely versatile piece of training equipment that can increase your hand speed and improve your striking ability. It's an especially effective tool for expanding your combination skills in close quarters, teaching you how to blend fists and elbows together in a blurring attack from all directions.

Many martial artists, particularly those from traditional backgrounds, have little or no experience with the speed bag. They generally strike the bag a few times and walk away in frustration. However, all martial artists can find the speed bag useful. It allows one to hone fighting combinations while practicing alone, without a training partner. The speed bag's unique rebounding action is a private tutor, yielding instant feedback about the effectiveness of your techniques—and with virtually no potential for injury.

Following are directions for proper use of the speed bag, as well as a number of training exercises to help you develop proficiency in your striking techniques.

When assuming the basic speed-bag stance, distance yourself so the bag will not strike your face on the rebound. The elbows should be out from the sides. The fists should move in continual small circles between eye and chin level when practicing on the speed bag. Use the same footwork you would when sparring.

Equipment

The speed bag is composed of three pieces of equipment: a rebound board, a swivel attachment and the bag itself. A modest unit can be purchased at most department or sporting-goods stores for $100.

Practitioners should be aware of several important factors about each piece of the speed bag. The rebound board supports the bag. Several types are available, or you can make your own. A heavier board is more resilient, won't rattle as much and yields a softer, lower sound.

A piece of plywood can be added to the top of lighter boards for reinforcement. Schools are better off with a heavy-duty professional model with a self-adjusting hand crank.

The speed bag's sound is an integral part of the training experience, but if quiet is a primary concern, metal rebound rings are available, although not recommended. Swivels come in three types: ball-hook, universal hinge and 360-degree ball bearing. Only advanced practitioners are able to discern a difference in swivel performance, but the ball-hook variety are easier for changing bags. It is important to keep the swivel screwed tightly. Any play in the swivel kills the natural bouncing of the bag.

Speed bags come in an assortment of shapes and sizes. Generally, larger, longer bags are slower and require more force. It is recommended to start with a medium-size bag, such as an 11-by-8-inch model. This size offers sufficient control and speed. Leave the 9-by-6-inch and 8-by-5-inch varieties, which are lightning fast, for advanced practitioners. Keep the bag inflated to its proper level. Less air makes it softer and slower; more air makes it faster and subject to an early blowout.

Bag gloves are optional but are recommended for unconditioned hands, particularly if striking a bag with hard external seams.

Rhythm 101

The speed bag allows you to link techniques together in fascinating combinations while developing speed and rhythm. The bag responds in relation to the striking force. Both fist and elbow strikes can be delivered from various angles: front or side, on an inward or outward path. Because the varying strikes determine the bag's direction, the direction constantly changes. The key, then, to bag control and successful combinations is understanding how bag direction and rhythm are intertwined.

The most important factor in developing rhythm is determining the direction of the next strike. A strike coming from the same general direction as the preceding one will always occur after an odd "beat" or number of

Martial artists can practice a wide array of techniques on the speed bag, including ridgehand strikes (1), elbow smashes (2) and kicks (3).

bounces: either one, three or five. Three is the usual number of bounces, and five is best for learning. The three-bounce rhythm creates a distinct sound, with the first rebound, directly off the fist, noticeably accented. This can be easily counted as one-two-three, one-two-three, with your strike always landing on the "one" beat. The same principle applies when using five beats. Therefore, when practicing repetitive backfists or ridgehands (which enter from the same direction) on the speed bag, always deliver them with three or five beats in between.

If delivering a follow-up strike in the opposite direction of your preceding technique, use an even number of rebounds, either two or four. For example, a right ridgehand/left ridgehand combination is accomplished with four bounces in between and is counted as one-two-three-four. If this combination is attempted after an odd number of beats, the speed bag will go in the same direction as the striking hand rather than toward it, which is incorrect.

Many technique combinations change the angle of attack several times, and there are some general rules for mixing directions. When a front strike is followed by a side strike (left backfist/right ridgehand, for example), an odd number of bounces is usually successful. When a side strike is followed by a front strike (left ridgehand/right straight punch), an even count works best. When mixing directions, however, individual differences can occur if your technique approaches the bag from a slightly different angle. For example, a side technique (ridgehand) may land more to the front or back side of the bag, altering the number of rebounds before your next strike. If you have trouble with a particular combination, try changing the count from even to odd or vice versa.

The bag's speed is determined by the amount of force used to strike it. Blast the bag hard, and it races out of control. It is more efficient to focus on fast rather than hard movements. As your techniques develop speed, not only will the bag move faster, but your strikes will feel more powerful. In fact, the speed bag helps teach the functional relationship of speed and power because controlled, rapid speed-bag striking is extremely powerful. Most people learn by counting the beats between strikes, but experience soon has them "feeling" the rhythm and hitting by sound. Direction changes create stutters in the rhythm much like musical syncopation. The sound of the bag repetitively hitting the board, with its accents and interbeats, adds to the practice experience.

When practicing, you will notice that the moving bag creates "after images"; the faster it goes, more images appear. To combat this phenom-

All hand strikes can be practiced on the speed bag, including the spinning backfist (1 and 2). Pretend you are delivering techniques in an actual fight, and develop a variety of combinations.

enon, focus the eyes on the center of the nonmoving bag, which is the general striking area.

Basic Stance

Adjust the height of the rebound board so the "belly" (the fattest part) of the bag is about level with your mouth (usually just below the brand name). It can be slightly higher or lower, higher being the better of the two choices. Distance yourself so your arms are bent at the elbows yet are far enough away so the bag will not strike your face on the rebound (don't laugh; this happens to everyone, but usually just once). The classic speed-bag stance is similar to a normal fighting posture, with the front of the body open, facing the bag. The elbows are raised out from the sides, and the upper arms are almost parallel to the floor. Anchor the hands close to the face, with the fists at the outside corner of each eye.

Striking Skills

To practice hand techniques (both front and side) on the speed bag, the fists should move in continual small circles between eye and chin level.

Lean into each strike, rotating the body, especially the shoulders. Elbow strikes are powered by the shoulders, circling in a short, crisp movement and ending with the fist at eye level. Aim for the belly of the bag. When the bag is moving, it is best to strike when it's angled slightly away from the straight position, thus avoiding a late strike. Pretend you are throwing actual fighting techniques, only in close quarters, and use the same footwork and movement you would when sparring. You will soon feel the correct body motion; don't fight it.

As mentioned earlier, the speed bag yields instant feedback about your technique. There is a crisp, sharp-sounding rebound and bag movement after a correct strike. A poor technique yields a weak-sounding rebound, and the bag will not fly in the intended direction, or it circles around the swivel. Late punches strike the bag from the bottom in an upward direction and are easily detected by the metallic sound of the swivel being driven upward. If your hands are slow, the bag will catch them after one rebound—just like an opponent would grab them.

"Breakdowns" (losses of control) invariably occur as part of the learning process. Most are caused by a few basic errors, such as "pawing" the bag in an up-and-down motion rather than striking into it, or overrotating the body by swinging the arms in exaggerated movements, which adds force and sends the bag out of control. These problems stem primarily from dropping the hands too low, then swinging them upward in an attempt to compensate. This can be remedied by maintaining proper position, using correct arm-swing mechanics and slowing down. Control is the key; speed follows automatically.

All hand and elbow strikes can be practiced on the speed bag: backfists, straight punches, ridgehands, hammerfists, knifehands, jabs, hooks, and both inside and outside elbow smashes. Begin by performing the techniques individually with each arm, using an odd count, and working up to five or more repetitions. Then devise your own combinations in progressions of two, three and then four techniques. Be sure to develop both the right and left hands. It is recommended that you strike softly at first, with the bag barely reaching the required number of rebounds. Later, imagine the bag as a board; focus through it and strike.

Distance Training

The speed bag is perfect for distance training. Take a small step back, then spring forward to close the distance. To make it more difficult, let the bag swing slowly, so you must time your move exactly. You can also practice retreating techniques, delivering a backfist, ridgehand or side kick

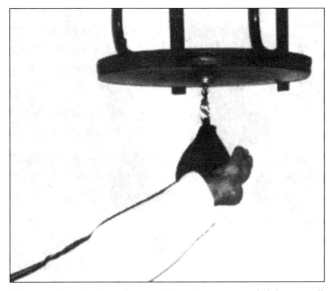

When practicing kicks on the speed bag, it is recommended that a small "S" hook be added to the swivel to extend the distance between your foot and the board.

while springing away from the bag.

You can also practice hitting the bag "freestyle," using no set rhythm. Swing the bag slowly while you duck, bob and weave, as if sparring. Let the bag bounce from two to six times while picking your shots by sight more than sound.

Because martial artists like to kick just about anything, the speed bag is an enticing target. When practicing kicks on the speed bag, it is highly recommended that you extend the distance between the board and your foot by using a longer bag or adding a small "S" hook to the swivel. Roundhouse, hook and crescent kicks can all be effectively practiced on the bag. The previously mentioned tips on rhythm apply to kicks, as well.

* * *

The speed bag can add variety and enjoyment to your training regimen. If you practice on it regularly, you will quickly reap its benefits and will soon need lightning rods for your hands. In a month or so, you'll be ready for multiple elbow/fist techniques—and the jump to warp speed.

DOUBLE DRAGON SHAOLIN KUNG FU
Mysterious *Mi Zong* Style Is at the Art's Core

by Jeffrey J. Kelly • Photos by Greg Peterson • September 1991

The year was 1953. The place: one of the many docks that surround the coastal city of Hong Kong. Security guards kept close watch on the passengers as they disembarked from the large steamship. Bored with their assignments, the guards would often harass the timid passengers. Some even turned to extortion, squeezing goods and money from the poor peasants. One guard's eyes were drawn to a beautiful leather suitcase belonging to a middle-aged Chinese man. The guard looked the man over and decided he could easily be intimidated into giving up the bag.

The guard stepped in front of the man and demanded that the suitcase be turned over to him for "inspection." He was shocked when the man politely refused his order. Once more the guard demanded the bag, and again he was politely but firmly rebuffed. Unaccustomed to such resistance, the guard became angry and embarrassed.

Hoping to avert trouble, one of the disembarking passengers called to the guard: "Hey, don't you know who that is? That's the famous master of the double dragon system. You had better leave him alone or there will be trouble."

But the guard became even angrier. Fearful of losing face before the growing crowd, the guard screamed at the man to give him the bag, then lunged forward to grab it. The man, who had remained calm despite the guard's outbursts, suddenly leaped into action. Curling the fingers of his right hand into a "leopard's paw," he evaded the guard's attack and struck, seemingly without effort, in a sideways motion that caught the guard in the ribs. Those watching scarcely saw the older man move and were shocked when the guard crumpled to the ground. In the ensuing confusion, the man slipped into the crowd and disappeared. The guard was taken to his home and a doctor was summoned, but even after treatment the guard remained bedridden.

The next day, the guard received a surprising visit from the man who had hit him in the ribs. "I have brought you some medicine," the visitor said. "Please take it. If you do not, you will be dead within 24 hours."

The guard turned a deaf ear to the man's offer of help. The older man, saddened by the guard's foolish bravado, placed the medicine on a table and left. By the next day, the guard was dead.

Like most southern Chinese kung fu styles, *mi zong* is primarily hand-oriented and includes such techniques as the "leopard's paw" strike, elbow bridges and binding maneuvers.

* * *

The middle-aged man in the preceding story was Chen Qing-wang, and the technique he used to subdue the rapacious guard came from *jing wu guan* double dragon *Shaolin* kung fu. An unwieldy name, perhaps, but one that paid homage to all the systems Chen had mastered—except one. Conspicuously absent is the name of the art that was the core of jing wu guan: *mi zong* kung fu.

Chen got most of his martial arts training at Shanghai's famous Jing Wu Athletic Association, founded in the early 1900s by Huo Yuan-jia, one of the most famous martial arts figures in China's modern times. Hou had trained in mi zong since an early age, and he and the masters of four other arts created a synthesis that became known as jing wu guan. This system was composed of techniques and principles from the *er liang* (two elements) style, seven-star praying mantis, *wu*-style *tai chi chuan*, and mi zong. The composite style came about naturally when students at the athletic association began to study under more than one master. To this art, Chen added parts of other systems, such as double dragon and Shaolin kung fu.

Chen served with the nationalists against the communists during China's civil war, teaching his style to the troops. In 1949, he moved his family to Hong Kong and later handed down his art to his four sons. In keeping with

Chinese tradition, the oldest son, Chen Zuo-ming, received the complete system, while the other three received progressively less knowledge. Chen trained his sons in the traditional manner, sometimes known as "table kung fu." Seldom were there formal lessons; rather, the father would occasionally jump up from the dinner table and ask his sons, "Have you seen this?" He would then demonstrate a few movements, and it was up to the sons to go and practice on their own.

Chen's oldest son decided not to teach the family art to the public and instead elected to continue his medical practice. The second son, Chen Zuo-hui, was highly ranked in Japanese karate and in 1975 was asked by the Japanese *budokan* to move to Australia and open a school there. At first, he also refused to teach his father's jing wu guan to outsiders. It was in 1977, only after seeing the dearth of genuine kung fu in the area and fearful that the family system might be lost, that he began to accept jing wu guan students.

As Chen Zuo-hui taught his father's system, he also made some changes in it. Originally, the system contained five long empty-hand sets. Chen Zuo-hui broke these down into eight basic and three advanced sets. In this way, the forms were not as overwhelming and were more easily absorbed by the students. Chen Zuo-hui also introduced concepts from some of the other arts he had studied, adopting *muay Thai* kicking techniques and stressing footwork and mobility. All these innovations aside, the core of jing wu guan is still mi zong kung fu, which accounts for 60 percent of the system's techniques.

Mi zong, meaning "lost track," dates from the 13th century. Primarily a southern Chinese style, it is an excellent receiving and countering system. Like most southern Chinese styles, it is primarily hand-oriented. It includes such techniques as the "leopard's paw" fist, elbow bridges, and winding and binding maneuvers. Although mi zong relies primarily on the horse stance, it also allows practitioners mobility.

Separating the mi zong techinques from the rest of jing wu guan might seem like an impossible task, but Greg Peterson of Australia is determined to try. Peterson began his jing wu guan training soon after Chen Zuo-hui opened the doors of his Sydney-based school in 1977. Peterson attended classes six and sometimes seven days a week and recalls what the early training was like.

"The studio itself was dark and dingy," Peterson states. "The roof leaked and the room was too narrow. It was hot in the summer and cold in the winter. The training sessions would last for two hours at a stretch, with virtually no rest during a class. The training was hard, but the students all loved Chen Zuo-hui and would work themselves until they dropped. We were so enthusiastic that we used to literally stop traffic on the street below. People would gather and peer up at us on the second floor, trying to figure out what was going on. Even though the training could be brutal at times, we developed a strong sense of family."

Peterson trained with Chen Zuo-hui for four years and then began teaching on his own. Since founding his own school in 1981, Peterson has gone on to study several other martial arts, such as *jujutsu*, classical judo

Greg Peterson (above) learned *jing wu guan* kung fu from Chen Zuo-hui and now teaches the style to students in Australia.

and, most recently, *Shaolin chuan*. While studying in a training center near the legendary Shaolin Temple in China's Henan province, Peterson had the rare opportunity to become a 31st-generation lay disciple of the temple. Peterson considers his exposure to genuine Shaolin chuan and his friendship with the temple monks to be the most illuminating experience of his martial arts career.

"When I was studying jing wu guan," he says, "we were given one application for every movement in the set. After coming back from China and going over my jing wu guan sets again, I realized that there are actually several possible applications for each move, so that, in a 36-movement set, there are literally hundreds of applications. Many of the techniques are quite subtle, but if the student knows how to properly investigate the system, he will find that it is virtually without limits." Inspired by his experience overseas, Peterson has begun re-examining jing wu guan and is attempting to track down the pure mi zong that is the core of the system.

"Mi zong is a complete system," he says. "It contains everything one could possibly need. Although it is a traditional art and I approach it in a traditional manner, I find that the art has no boundary as long as the individual has no boundary."

For Peterson, being a traditionalist does not exclude studying other martial arts or developing innovations on his own. Based on his investigation of body mechanics, he has created his own unique kicking style, which is both economical and powerful. His studio in Albion Park, Australia, offers classes in jujutsu and white crane kung fu, both taught by qualified teachers, and Peterson hopes to add the Philippine art *arnis* to the curriculum soon. By offering other arts, Peterson hopes to keep alive the spirit of the original Jing Wu Athletic Association, which produced some of modern China's greatest martial artists.

*   *   *

The lineage of traditional mi zong kung fu remains unbroken: from Hou Yuan-jia and the Shanghai Jing Wu Athletic Association through Chen Qing-wang and his sons to a new generation of western students determined to preserve and further this rare martial art. For Peterson, studying and imparting the wisdom of traditional mi zong is his life's practice, one that, like the search for self-knowledge, is without boundaries and without limits.

KAJUKENBO HAND STRIKES
Brutally Effective on the Street and in Tournaments
by Jane Hallander • Photos by Jane Hallander • October 1991

*K*ajukenbo is one of the most practical martial arts in the world, with training so real that, years ago in Hawaii, kajukenbo instructors locked the school doors at the beginning of each training session. This served two purposes: It kept the students from escaping the brutal training, and it kept visitors outside, hiding the training from public view.

Kajukenbo was founded in Hawaii during World War II. Its creator, Adriano Emperado, was a student of *kempo* karate instructor William Chow. Emperado incorporated other martial arts such as judo, *jujutsu, tang soo do* and Chinese boxing into his practical, self-defense-oriented kajukenbo system. After the war, Hawaiian martial artists Al Dacascos, Tony Ramos, Aleju Reyes and Joe Halbuna brought kajukenbo to the mainland United States and spread the art throughout the West Coast.

Over the years, kajukenbo has developed a reputation for producing talented tournament fighters. One of these fighters is San Jose, California-based kajukenbo practitioner Richard Barefield, who won the sparring grand championship at Ed Parker's 1987 International Karate Championships. According to Barefield, it's kajukenbo's highly effective hand techniques that set it apart from other martial arts. "It doesn't matter whether you use them for self-defense or tournament semicontact sparring, kajukenbo's hand techniques suit everyone—man or woman, large or small," Barefield says.

Kajukenbo's hand techniques are simple and direct, making them easy to practice and easy to use. The kajukenbo reverse punch, for example,

Richard Barefield (left) demonstrates the use of the *kajukenbo* reverse-punch counter. Barefield first blocks (1) an incoming punch, then counters (2) with a reverse punch to the opponent's midsection.

moves out and back in a straight line, making it equally useful for competition or self-defense.

The reverse punch is a popular finishing technique for kajukenbo stylists in self-defense situations. Kajukenbo tactics call for an initial block, then a takedown or joint break. If the opponent starts the confrontation with a punch, the kajukenbo practitioner counters by first blocking the strike, and then he might follow with a grab and wrist lock, armbar or bone-breaking maneuver. After the opponent is forced to the ground, the reverse punch is often used to finish the encounter and render the opponent incapacitated.

Sometimes, a self-defense situation calls for a reverse punch as the initial counter-technique. In these instances, Barefield likes to target the opponent's solar plexus, which is one of the body's most vulnerable areas, no matter how big or small the adversary is. Once the opponent is stunned by the reverse punch, the kajukenbo stylist follows with a stronger technique, such as a knee break followed by a takedown.

"Assuming the opponent attacks you, your family or your property, you have the right to defend yourself," Barefield says. "Kajukenbo was originally designed as the complete solution to any kind of attack. The degree of force you use depends on the type of attack and whether or not the attacker has a weapon."

The kajukenbo reverse punch is also a useful weapon in tournament sparring. Barefield prefers to employ the technique as a counter after enticing the opponent into a compromising position. For instance, Barefield may put his lead hand down, inviting the opponent to launch an attack toward his head. Once the opponent has lowered his defenses and initiated his attack, Barefield moves in with a full-power reverse punch to the solar

Barefield is then in position to apply (3) a wrist lock and take his adversary to the ground (4).

Demonstrating *kajukenbo's* inner-ridgehand technique, Richard Barefield blocks (1) an assailant's punch and counters (2) with an inner-ridgehand strike to the bridge of the nose.

plexus. This technique works well as a counter to most attacks, even against a rear-leg roundhouse kick, which loses its effectiveness once Barefield closes the distance.

Body punches are never pulled at Barefield's school, even in sparring practice. Kajukenbo theory states that, because you wouldn't pull a punch in a street situation, you shouldn't pull one in practice, either. Obviously, this kind of realistic training makes kajukenbo fighters quick to hone their defensive techniques.

"It doesn't matter whether you use them for self-defense or tournament semicontact sparring, kajukenbo's hand techniques suit everyone—man or woman, large or small."
—Richard Barefield

Kajukenbo reverse-punch fists are made by wrapping the thumb around the first two knuckles of the hand. The thumb acts as a brace, keeping the fist together while protecting the hand. The striking surface for the reverse punch is the flat part of the fist between the first and second knuckles.

A firm stance is also important when delivering a reverse punch, according to Barefield. "A sloppy stance leads to a sloppy reverse punch," he says.

Barefield recommends using the reverse punch in conjunction with proper footwork. Never simply lead with the punch. Always step first and let the punch follow your body and footwork.

Barefield follows (3) with an elbow lock, taking (4) his opponent down.

The kajukenbo reverse punch should not be confused with a straight punch. Reverse punches get their name from the act of pulling the punching hand back to the body. Straight punches, conversely, are left extended for a longer time. Keeping the punching arm extended is dangerous, however, leaving you unprotected and slow to react to your opponent's next move.

Another effective kajukenbo hand technique is the inner-ridgehand strike. The striking surface for this technique is the side of the hand, between the end of the thumb joint and the beginning of the wrist. Keep your thumb along the side of your hand, not bent under the palm. If you bend it, you can easily break your thumb when striking. Using the thumb as a brace along the side of the hand makes the hand stronger.

As self-defense tools, inner-ridgehand techniques generally follow initial blocks and are employed as counterattacks to the assailant's nose or throat. They are particularly effective when delivered to soft, sensitive parts of the body.

For sparring competition, inner-ridgehand strikes often target the back of the opponent's head. Again, Barefield recommends setting up the technique by offering the opponent an open target. Once the opponent commits, the kajukenbo stylist parries the attack and counters with an inner-ridgehand strike. Even if he doesn't score with the ridgehand, the kajukenbo practitioner is in position to immediately follow up with another hand technique, usually a reverse punch.

A third kajukenbo hand technique is the backfist. This straight backfist should not be confused with "blind" spinning backfists that do not allow you to see your opponent until after the technique is executed. Spinning backfists are risky because the opponent may see your intention and

Demonstrating *kajukenbo's* backfist technique, Richard Barefield (left) faces off (1) with an opponent and sidesteps (2) a punch, countering with a backfist to the temple and reverse punch (3) to the jaw. Barefield then applies (4) a painful armbar technique, taking (5) his opponent to the ground.

counterattack before you see him. Plus, because you cannot accurately judge the distance to your opponent, it is difficult to control the amount of force used in a spinning backfist, making it a dangerous technique for tournament competition.

For self-defense purposes, the straight backfist often targets the attacker's temple. The striking surface is the first two knuckles. A good follow-up maneuver is a reverse punch to the throat.

Tournament backfists require more timing than speed. Most competitors will have their lead hand up, protecting against a backfist. But as they deliver their own attack, their lead hand unconsciously slips down, allowing the kajukenbo stylist to counter with a straight backfist. If, for example, the opponent launches a reverse punch, his body dips downward and his lead hand slips down as well, leaving an opening for a backfist to the temple.

The backfist can also be used to set up other techniques. By delivering repeated backfists to the head, the opponent becomes conditioned to blocking high, leaving him vulnerable to mid- and low-level techniques, such as a roundhouse kick.

*　　*　　*

Although kajukenbo is composed of joint locks, throws, kicks and numerous ground-fighting maneuvers, it is the three aforementioned hand techniques—reverse punch, inner ridgehand and straight backfist—which often determine whether you have an opportunity to make use of any of kajukenbo's other defenses.

OKINAWAN KARATE'S PRINCIPLE OF CONTINUOUS ATTACK
Strike and Strike Again Until the Opponent Is Finished

by William Durbin • August 1992

Renzoku ken (continuous fist) is an ancient combat principle developed in Okinawa. Although it is still found today in some *shorin-ryu* and *goju-ryu* karate schools, few practice the maneuver as it was originally developed by the warriors of Okinawa.

These warriors practiced an art called *bushi-te*, which was designed to allow them to defend themselves in any situation. They were less of a standing army for repelling invaders and more of a peacekeeping force to deal with criminals and provide security for the king. Thus, the art they practiced needed to meet various criteria.

First, the art had to have excellent grappling applications for use in subduing and restraining prisoners. Next, it needed to include the devastating *ikken* (one-strike kill) technique for life-or-death situations. It also addressed vital-point strikes so the warriors would know where to deliver blows that could severely injure or kill an attacker. And finally, for those situations when grappling was ineffective and the one-strike kill was foiled, the art provided a follow-up attack known as renzoku ken.

Renzoku ken is a process in which basic techniques of ikken are expanded so that, if the first strike is unable to stop an attack, the defender follows up immediately with a natural flow of techniques. When *kenpo* karate was first brought to the United States, the art's most noticeable attribute was renzoku ken, so much so that as American styles developed, many were shaped around this principle. Yet the biggest complaint levied against these systems has been that the techniques that compose the renzoku ken series lack focus.

In the bushi-te practiced by ancient Okinawan warriors, each renzoku ken technique was fully focused, as if it were the only technique needed. If the technique was blocked or dodged, the bushi-te stylist would flow into another technique that was a natural extension of the original movement. The result was an extremely effective series of techniques that kept an attacker on the defensive and eventually overpowered him.

Renzoku ken serves as an effective follow-up maneuver to a grappling technique. The Okinawan warriors realized that, if their grappling moves failed, they would be in close proximity to their opponent and vulnerable

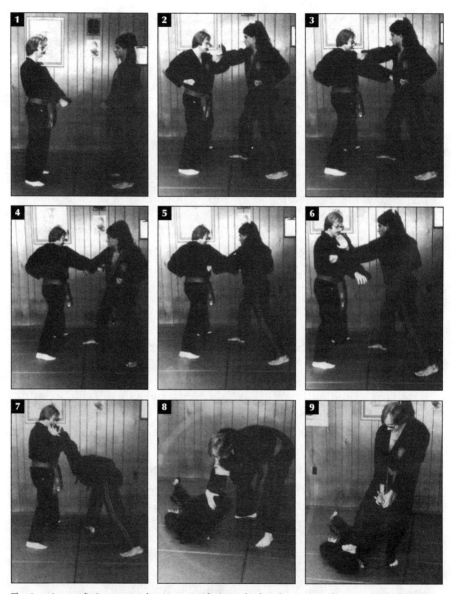

The "continuous fist" concept takes into consideration the fact that it may take more than one strike to defeat your attacker. Faced (1) with an opponent, the Okinawan karate stylist (left) deflects (2) a punch and counters (3) with a reverse punch that is blocked (4). The aggressor launches a second punch (5), which the Okinawan stylist deflects (6) with a double side block, allowing him to flow into an elbow lock (7). The defender then spins (8) the attacker to the mat, finishing (9) with a reverse wrist lock and head stomp.

to a counterattack. Thus, the bushi-te exponent was prepared to transition naturally from the grappling technique to a withering barrage of strikes. Students can practice this maneuver by using a drill known as *toide*, in which one person attacks while the defender applies a joint lock, then flows into whatever counterstrike comes most naturally. Students can take the drill a step further and conduct a give-and-take session, whereby several techniques are exchanged before a final resolution is achieved.

Kiyojute-ryu kenpo utilizes both the renzoku ken and toide training principles of bushi-te. And as in the ancient method, most of the training is performed in a freestyle manner. Generally, only the attacker's first move is planned, while the ensuing follow-up techniques flow naturally.

Renzoku ken can only enhance one's self-defense training. If a karate practitioner only practices ikken methods, he begins to believe that one strike is all that is necessary to end a real confrontation. All too often, however, it is the second or third strike that actually ends an altercation on the street, thus the importance of renzoku ken training.

One's body posture dictates the follow-up techniques used in renzoku ken; the practitioner should deliver any blow that can be freely employed. The defender should cease his counterattack if and when the attacker gives up the fight. Some karate systems include striking combinations that do not follow natural body movement and direct students to carry each technique through to the end of the series. If, however, a movement is not a natural extension of the practitioner's previous maneuver, it probably will not be effective and could put the defender into a precarious situation. More important, if the practitioner continues a series of self-defense strikes after his attacker has either capitulated or is incapable of further aggression, he has (according to the laws of most states) become the aggressor and can be charged accordingly. Your right to defend yourself ends when an attacker has halted his aggression.

It is therefore important to learn not only how to follow up your initial defense but also how to stop at the appropriate time. This is one reason why freestyle renzoku ken practice is so valuable.

Renzoku ken is one of the most important principles of the ancient Okinawan martial arts and has greatly influenced the development of American combat systems. When learned properly, renzoku ken will allow modern martial artists to respond with the same effectiveness enjoyed by the ancient Okinawan warriors of bushi-te.

KALI'S UNARMED COMBAT TECHNIQUES
Defanging the Snake With Your Hands, Elbows and Knees

by Tom Barell • Photos by Tom Barell • November 1992

The Philippine art *kali* is composed of numerous principles, all of which are based on the style's weapons systems. Among these principles is a concept called "defanging the snake." In order to disarm an opponent, kali practitioners will strike their opponent's weapon-wielding hand with a stick or other device, thus removing the adversary's "poisonous fangs" and rendering him harmless.

Although the concept of "defanging the snake" is most commonly employed when the practitioner is armed with one of kali's many weapons, it can be easily applied to unarmed combat as well. Just as kali stylists believe that any weapon is simply an extension of the hand, so too is the hand or arm a weapon in and of itself, and it can be employed in the same manner as most of kali's weapons. This empty-hand form of kali is referred to as *gunting*.

Gunting means "scissor" and refers to the motion of a common kali knife-disarming technique. The idea is to destroy or immobilize the opponent's limbs—especially any limb holding a weapon. If you can destroy your opponent's limb, you render him harmless, just like the defanged snake. If your opponent is unable to strike you with his arms or legs, you have an obvious advantage.

Gunting techniques require minimal effort yet can seriously weaken your opponent, cause him confusion and incapacitate him. The following are brief discussions of how these empty-hand techniques work against an opponent's punching and kicking attacks.

Gunting Techniques vs. Punches

There are two types of gunting techniques from which to choose when defending against an opponent's high punch: primary and secondary. Primary gunting maneuvers are the more damaging of the two and should only be executed when your hands are in an "on-guard" position. Secondary gunting techniques are more suitable when your hands are at your sides. All gunting maneuvers are centered around the principles of "economy of motion" and "feasibility."

The most effective primary gunting maneuver against an opponent's straight punch is the "vertical elbow" technique. This move can be executed

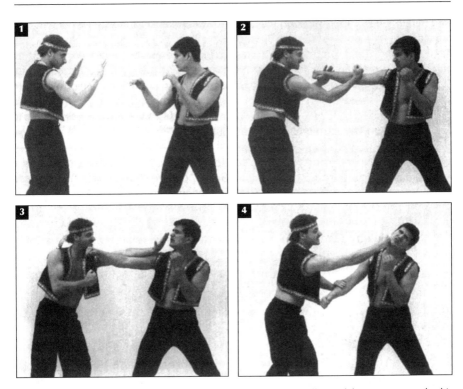

In *kali's* "basic horizontal" gunting maneuver, the defender (left) faces off (1) with his opponent, and as his foe delivers a right-hand punch, the kali practitioner deflects the blow and counters (2-4) with a biceps punch/eye jab/backfist combination.

with either your front or rear elbow and can break your opponent's punching hand. It is a simple technique to perform and requires minimal effort. From an on-guard position, you guide your opponent's fist into the damaging tip of your elbow. Your elbow remains in tight and in a vertical position during the technique, minimizing any deviation from the on-guard position. When executed properly, this technique can set the stage for the entire fight and turn an aggressive opponent into one who is wary of attacking.

Even more damaging than the vertical elbow gunting is the "horizontal elbow" technique. This elbow gunting can generate more power from the hips, resulting in more destruction to the opponent's limb. The technique requires more of a commitment, making it somewhat dangerous to deliver, but if timed correctly, it can practically guarantee total destruction of the opponent's limb.

Another effective although difficult technique is the "scissor" gunting, better known as the "basic horizontal" maneuver. Like most gunting techniques, it is derived from a kali knife maneuver. There are three strikes involved in this technique: a hammerfist to the biceps, a finger jab to the eyes and a backfist to the temple. The movements often resemble the cutting motion of scissors, hence the technique's name. The biceps is one of the muscles responsible for extending the arm to execute a punch. Damaging the biceps with a hammerfist will slow your opponent's punches considerably. This technique is often used for bridging the gap between punching range and trapping range, and therefore involves essential footwork. Most primary gunting techniques are immediately followed by a counterattack or even multiple gunting maneuvers to assure total destruction of the opponent's attacking limb.

Secondary gunting techniques are used when you are the victim of a surprise attack or if your hands are poorly positioned when attacked. For example, if an opponent delivers a straight punch while your hands are down, you should respond with a secondary gunting maneuver. The term "secondary" simply means the response is not your first choice but the best choice at the time. Successfully executing a primary gunting technique while your hands are down requires above-average physical attributes.

Secondary gunting techniques often resemble sweeping motions to the inside, to the outside or upward. One hand will deflect the opponent's punch, while the other hand forms a fist and strikes in a whiplike fashion to the attacker's biceps or ulnar nerve (funny bone). The choice of targets depends on whether you are sweeping to the inside or to the outside. These techniques are therefore typically referred to as "inside guntings" and "outside guntings," and they occur on a horizontal plane.

Both inside and outside gunting techniques require lateral footwork in order to avoid an opponent's combination attack. When it is not feasible to move laterally, an "upward gunting" technique is the answer. The upward gunting maneuver is a vertical sweeping motion that always strikes the attacker's funny bone. Because of the direction of the strike and in order to avoid a combination attack, it is necessary to lower your elevation. Because a drop in elevation can leave you stationary, it is wise to drop your knee on your opponent's forward foot as you lower yourself.

Secondary gunting techniques are bothersome to your opponent. If followed by a primary technique, secondary gunting maneuvers can incapacitate your opponent's punching prowess.

Gunting Techniques vs. Kicks

Any kick the opponent delivers below the waist and in a circular pattern can be destroyed by your knee. Targets include the opponent's instep or

The most effective *kali* response to an opponent's punch is the "vertical elbow" technique. In the series above, kali stylist Tom Barell (left) faces off (1) with an adversary who delivers a right-hand punch. Barell counters (2) with a rear vertical elbow smash to the opponent's fist.

lower shin area. This gunting technique requires little effort, but in order to avoid injury to yourself, there are a few points to remember.

Because your forward knee is used to destroy all incoming kicks, to insure stability it may be necessary to pivot toward the opponent's kick to get an accurate shot at him. You must also make sure that your knee is completely bent and directly facing the target. The knee is strong when bent but weak when extended.

A linear kick to your midsection, such as the side kick, can be stopped with either your knee or your elbow, depending on the kick's height. In most cases, an elbow technique is more suitable. The tip of your forward elbow will drop vertically onto the ankle of your opponent's kicking leg. Your rear hand helps guide the kick downward to the ground. If the kick is thrown a little higher, disregard the elbow strike and instead bring your forward knee up into the opponent's inner ankle. In order to stay balanced, you will need to lean back as you deliver the knee strike.

High, circular kicks to the face, such as the roundhouse, crescent and spinning hook kicks, can be destroyed with your elbows. Targets are the opponent's instep or lower shin. These elbow strikes are executed just like you would deliver a vertical elbow gunting against an opponent's punch. The only major difference is that you must face the direction of the kick while guiding it into your elbow. This will add enormous power to the technique.

Kick destruction techniques are nearly always followed by a counter-kick, usually to your opponent's planted leg. Without a good base to stand on, your opponent becomes stagnant and easier to hit.

*   *   *

Whether used against an opponent's punch or kick, kali's empty-hand techniques have the potential to set the stage for the entire fight. By slowing and altering the rhythm of your opponent's attacks, you gain the advantage and quickly change an attacker into a defender. With minimal effort, you can destroy his arsenal and drastically alter his fight plans. Map out your strategy, choose your path and use kali's empty-hand techniques as your steppingstones to victory.

KARATE'S FORGOTTEN CIRCULAR PUNCHES
Classical *Kata* Contain Curved as Well as Linear Strikes

by James R. Melton • Photos by Wanda Melton • January 1993

Rules govern the strategies, and thus the techniques, a competitor uses to win any game, and the sport of tournament sparring is no exception. Because of the nature of sparring—namely, scoring on your opponent before he can score on you while simultaneously limiting your vulnerability—tournament fighting is a high-speed game of tag fought at relatively long range. This makes for an exciting, relatively safe game of fast reflexes and excellent hand/eye/foot coordination.

Unfortunately, in the last 20 years, many competitors and instructors seem to have concentrated exclusively on those aspects and techniques that were easiest to apply in the game of tournament sparring. This questionable picking and choosing of techniques was accompanied in many schools by a de-emphasis of traditional *kata* (prearranged training sequences). Some instructors have gone so far as to create new kata, which are no more than a combination of sparring techniques, second-rate gymnastics and Sunday-morning *Kung Fu Theater*. Students coming up through this type of system end up with a very narrow view of karate in terms of tactics and techniques.

Consequently, some practitioners believe that, in order to learn techniques such as uppercuts, hooks, roundhouse or overhand punches, it is necessary to go outside karate to other sources such as boxing. Nothing could be further from the truth. Traditional kata offer a wider variety of circular techniques than most practitioners are aware of.

Following is an analysis of four common close-range circular karate punches, the classical kata in which they can be found, and how they can be applied in both tournament sparring and self-defense.

Uppercut

The uppercut (*ura zuki*) is found in the *heian godan, bassai dai, seiunchin* and several other kata practiced by *shoto-kan, shito-ryu, goju-ryu* and other stylists. The technique varies slightly, however, in each kata. In heian godan, an uppercut is applied in conjunction with an inside block from a cross-legged stance. In bassai dai, a block with the leg is followed by a double punch (*yama zuki*), which consists of an overhand strike to the face and an uppercut to the body. In seiunchin, the practitioner steps in, grabs his opponent's arm and pulls downward while delivering an uppercut to the chin.

The textbook version of the uppercut begins with the practitioner's punching hand near his waist and his elbow bent about 90 degrees. The punch is delivered with an upward rotation of the arm at the shoulder, while the elbow remains bent and brushes along the side of the practitioner as the punching arm goes upward. The forearm and fist can remain palm-up, or a snapping motion may be used. In either case, the arm motion must be coordinated with the hips and legs to generate maximum power. The height and the angle of the target will determine where along the punch's path contact should take place.

Uppercuts are best applied to targets that are tilted toward the puncher, or facing downward. An opponent leaning forward at close range, for example, is presenting his torso and face at the correct angle to be hit with an uppercut. An opponent standing upright in close range with his chin up is presenting his chin as an uppercut target. The uppercut is also a useful weapon against an opponent who ducks forward to avoid attacks to the head or against a taller adversary who has allowed you into fighting range.

Hook Punch

Hook punches (*kagi zuki*) are found in several classical kata such as the *tekki* and *jion* forms. In both kata, the hook punch is applied from a side stance along a line parallel with an imaginary line under the practitioner's feet. The punch is stopped at the edge of the body with the forearm angled

The *seiunchin* form, found in a number of classical karate styles, includes a technique (1-2) in which the practitioner uses one hand to grab and pull downward on an opponent's punch while simultaneously delivering an uppercut.

The scissors punch (1) consists of two roundhouse strikes to the body and is found in the *chinte* and *wankan* *kata*. The practitioner uses (2) one hand to block and grab and the other to punch with.

slightly downward and the elbow bent approximately 90 degrees. In the jion kata, the hook punch is also executed as one-half of a double punch. A virtually identical double punch is also found in the *kanku sho* and *bassai sho* kata, but the hook punch portion of the twin technique is carried past the edge of the body. The goal of the hook punch in classical kata is to hit a target that is very close to the puncher, but one which is facing at a right angle to and is more or less even with the edge of the puncher's body. In this position, the punch must be delivered on a line parallel with an imaginary line drawn through the puncher's hips to the target. For the punch to be effective, the shoulders must rotate slightly in order for the elbow to be positioned correctly behind and in line with the wrist, knuckles and target. Beginners are taught to begin the punch with their hand near their waist. The forearm slides along the practitioner's side until the elbow clears the body, then the forearm starts to rotate palm-down. The punch is pulled across the body by using a combination of waist rotation and the chest muscles. The most common mistake practitioners make during this technique is not allowing the elbow to move out and around far enough so that there is proper alignment of the elbow, wrist, knuckles and target at the moment of impact. The hook punch is particularly useful as a counterattack following a side-step motion. Hook punches can also be applied at grappling range, where straight punches are generally ineffective.

Roundhouse Punch

A punch that follows a curved path to the target is called a roundhouse punch (*mawashi zuki*). A version of this punch, performed as one-half of a double punch, is found in both the *chinte* and *wankan* kata. In both classical forms, the practitioner turns and lowers his stance and then simultaneously punches the opponent in both sets of ribs. This twin technique is called a "scissors punch" (*hasami zuki*).

In the most basic version of the roundhouse punch, the practitioner's punching hand begins at his side and moves in a half circle from the hips, first outward, then inward. The elbow on the punching arm should be kept close to the practitioner's side for as long as possible. If the target is low, the path of the punch will be fairly level or parallel to the ground. If the target is higher or the purpose of the punch is to go over and/or around an obstacle such as an arm or shoulder, the trajectory of the punch will be more vertical. In order to punch vertically and still use the forearm and the armpit muscles correctly, the shoulders and hips must be twisted to bring the arm up, rather than lifting the arm separately from the shoulder.

The wrist, knuckles and elbow must be correctly aligned when striking the target with a roundhouse punch. The fist will hit the target palm-down in the horizontal version of the punch but will tilt more in the semivertical version. In the most extreme vertical version of the technique, the thumb is facing downward. Because of the position of the punching hand, it is not practical to bring this last punch straight over. The overhand punch, described next, would be a better choice because of the hand position on impact.

The roundhouse punch is particularly useful for punching around an opponent's block or other obstructions. An opponent who has chosen to protect the front of his body is leaving openings on the sides. A block

The double-punch technique (1) is found in the *shotokan* form *bassai dai*. In application (2) against an opponent, the defender uses his lower hand to block while delivering an overhand punch to the face with his upper hand.

appropriate for a straight punch often will not work against a curved punch to the same target, meaning the roundhouse punch is more difficult for the opponent to block. Typically, roundhouse punches are used at somewhat closer range than straight punches.

Overhand Punch

An example of the overhand punch is found in the bassai dai kata as part of a double punch. As one hand delivers an uppercut to the body, the other hand simultaneously attacks the opponent's face with an overhand punch.

To deliver the overhand punch, face the opponent in a cat stance, then depress your front shoulder slightly and direct the upper arm and shoulder of the punching arm upward and forward in a slight arc. The elbow of the punching arm must be bent in order for the knuckles, wrist and elbow to be correctly aligned at the point of impact. At the moment of impact, the fist is palm-down. A common error practitioners make when delivering this punch is to slide their forward hip joint backward to achieve the necessary tilt of the torso, rather than pushing the rear edge of their body up and over slightly, which drives their hand into the target with power supplied by the rear hip muscles and rear leg.

Like roundhouse techniques, an overhand punch is useful for going over an opponent's block or guard. It is also a way to avoid punching an opponent in the teeth and cutting your hand, which can happen with a straight punch to the face.

*   *   *

If a karate practitioner looks deep enough, he will discover all he needs to know about self-defense and effective sparring techniques in the classical kata. Not only do these ancient forms offer standard linear punches, but on closer inspection, practitioners also will discover that they contain many circular strikes. It is up to today's karate stylists to make sure that these time-honored maneuvers are passed on to the next generation of students.

SIX-HARMONIES KUNG FU
Strike Hard, Strike First and Strike Again Until the Opponent Goes Down

by Carlos Aldrete and Mark V. Wiley • Photos by Mark V. Wiley • March 1993

"Southern hands, northern legs" is a popular saying in kung fu circles and aptly illustrates the essence of the "southern six harmonies" kung fu style.

Southern six harmonies (*liu ho*) is an external kung fu system and should not be confused with its northern counterpart, "six harmonies and eight methods" (*liu hop pa fa*), which is an internal kung fu system. Liu ho focuses on infighting skills and is practiced primarily in China's Fukien province and in Taiwan. In contrast to its northern cousin, southern six-harmonies kung fu emphasizes hand techniques and contains just four kicks.

History of Liu Ho

According to Taiwan native Wu Chun Ying, liu ho is also known as *chai chuan* and was introduced to the Taiwanese by Chen Tsu, who is Wu's instructor. Chen began teaching liu ho in Taiwan during the Chinese cultural revolution, when thousands fled the mainland to what was then Formosa. Liu ho bears a close resemblance to Fukien white crane kung fu and the five-ancestors system, and shares stances, weapons and various training drills with both styles.

Fighting Principles

According to Wu, the "six harmonies" designation in liu ho refers to six factors (three internal and three external) that must work in unison for a practitioner to achieve proficiency in the system. The three internal factors are energy (*jin*), spirit (*shen*) and the mind (*yi*). The three external factors are the eyes (*yen*), hands (*sou*) and breath (*chi*).

Simplicity is the strength of southern six-harmonies kung fu. Through constant practice and perfection of many seemingly basic techniques, the liu ho stylist is able to transform these maneuvers into advanced applications. Consider, for example, a close-range double-palm strike to the opponent's chest. An average, unrefined double-palm strike will merely push an opponent or leave a surface bruise. But if the practitioner perfects his stance, is properly "rooted" and effectively applies his jin, the double-palm strike can be devastating. Even if the opponent has his guard up, the strike's "shock waves" will penetrate the body and injure the organs.

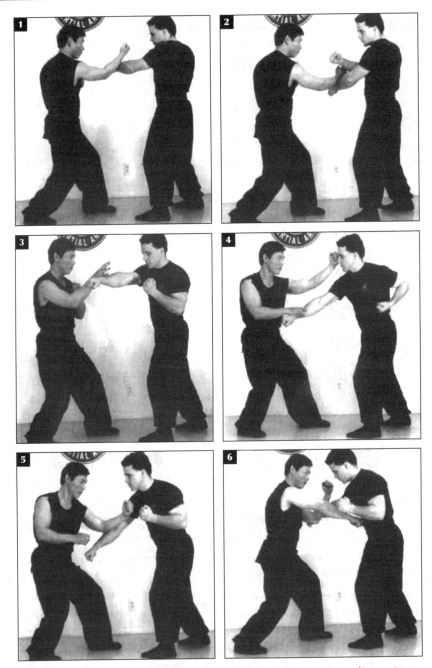

"Knocking at the door" is a six-harmonies kung fu method of interpreting and/or sensing an opponent's movements. In the sequence above, six-harmonies practitioner Wu Chun Ying (left) blocks (1) an attacker's punch and redirects it downward (2). Wu then intercepts (3) a right punch and pulls (4) his assailant into a back-knuckle strike to the nose. Wu forces (5) his foe's punching arm down with his left elbow, then finishes (6) with a "sinking punch" to the midsection.

The principal goal of six-harmonies kung fu is to improve your foundation, which will ultimately allow you to destroy an opponent's stability. It is for this reason that the system is almost devoid of kicking techniques. By employing light, evasive footwork coupled with a solid stance, the liu ho practitioner is able to quickly outmaneuver, control and defeat his adversary.

Another key liu ho tactic is the effective use of both "hard" and "soft" movements. The liu ho practitioner utilizes soft, evasive maneuvers against a stronger opponent and hard, powerful blows against a weaker adversary.

The six-harmonies stylist always seeks to close the distance between himself and his opponent as soon as possible, then proceeds to attack his foe with a barrage of blows. Often, liu ho blocks and strikes blend into one simultaneous defensive offensive technique. Every liu ho block is capable of being converted into a pulling or pushing technique. Each strike is intended to seriously injure the opponent. If the opponent blocks a blow, the liu ho practitioner immediately delivers another strike. Even if the opponent fails to block the initial strike, and it lands with full force, it is still followed by a second technique. Liu ho attacks do not cease until the opponent is knocked down. While attacking, the liu ho stylist always seeks to keep his elbows tucked in front of his torso to protect vital areas.

Generally, liu ho stylists attempt to avoid force-to-force confrontations with an opponent. This "hard" blocking method is used, however, if the liu ho practitioner is confident that his power is greater than that of his opponent. Properly applied, this force-to-force tactic can jar the opponent's body, allowing the liu ho stylist to seize the advantage.

The state of tension in a practitioner's body leads to yet another interpretation of southern six-harmonies' concept of hard and soft. The liu ho stylist's body should be relaxed (soft) before the initiation of an attack but becomes hard as iron on impact with the target. When meeting an attack, the liu ho practitioner's shoulders should be kept down and the chest slightly concave. This draws the opponent's body toward the liu ho stylist, where it is met with an explosive strike. This method of defense is known as "sucking in and spitting out."

Six-harmonies kung fu stylists attempt to strike first and remain on the offensive in order to stay a step ahead of their opponent. As they employ their attacking methods, liu ho practitioners are searching for the most efficient means of defeating their opponents. This is achieved by interpreting or "feeling" the opponent's reactions. This method of attack is known as "knocking on the door" or "asking for directions."

Another liu ho tactic involves maintaining constant pressure on the opponent after neutralizing his initial attack. A volley of rapid-fire blows, delivered from a variety of angles, will keep the opponent off-balance until he is knocked down. The six-harmonies stylist strives to develop a nonsubmissive attitude; even in retreat, he is committed to turning every defense into an attack. In order to maintain constant pressure on an opponent, the liu ho practitioner relies heavily on elusive footwork, dodging and sidestepping his adversary's attacks as he sets up for counter-techniques.

Training

Southern six-harmonies kung fu training is arduous. Initial training involves relentless practice of the system's four stances: horse stance (*bei bo*); empty-step stance (*hee bo*), hill-climbing stance (*ghi bo*) and three-wars stance (*sam chien*).

Emphasis is placed on the development of the three-wars stance, the style's trademark, in which 60 percent of the practitioner's weight is placed on the rear leg. The three-wars stance allows the practitioner superb mobility yet enables him to generate maximum power while retaining impeccable balance. Liu ho stylists often stomp the ground when utilizing this stance during forward or backward movement. This curious act serves several purposes: It acts as a stabilizing mechanism, it often disturbs an opponent's concentration, and it helps generate added power because of the "rebound" effect created by the ground.

Power in six-harmonies kung fu originates from the practitioner's feet, is generated from the waist and is released through the arms. Three types of energy are developed through the stylist's strange stomping action: straight-line, one-inch and jarring energy.

Six-harmonies kung fu places emphasis on developing the attributes necessary to "feel" or "listen" to an opponent's energy. To accomplish this, the liu ho stylist practices various two-person drills found in the system. "Iron body" and "iron forearm" training are also stressed to develop the practitioner's ability to withstand an opponent's attack.

The most common hand techniques in liu ho are the fist punch, palm strike, crane's wing blow and crane's head strike. In training their hands, six-harmonies stylists focus on double strikes, simultaneous attack and defense, and a variety of redirectional maneuvers that lead into joint locks and pressure-point strikes. To set up for a hand strike, the liu ho stylist often attempts to impede an opponent's arms while twisting, pushing or pulling his body off-balance.

During initial training, six-harmonies students perform movements as hard as possible. At later stages, however, they develop the ability to blend hard and soft maneuvers in a continuous, uninterrupted stream of motion.

After repeated practice, the liu ho practitioner learns to effectively combine the three internal and three external factors, achieving the ultimate goal of southern six-harmonies kung fu: the balance of hard and soft movements. When this level of development has been achieved, the liu ho practitioner has the ability to blend with his opponent's every move until choosing to end the confrontation.

In the self-defense sequence above, six-harmonies kung fu stylist Wu Chun Ying (right) squares off (1) against an opponent and deflects (2) a left punch. Wu then steps in with an elbow strike (3) to the ribs, followed by a back-knuckle strike (4) to the nose and crane wing strike (5) to the groin. Wu finishes by sweeping (6) his opponent's lead leg from the "retreating crane" posture.

KENPO KARATE'S THEORY OF REVERSE MOTION
Find the "Hidden" Strikes in Your Fighting Techniques

by Scott Clevenger • Photos by Scott Clevenger • August 1993

"For every action, there is an equal and opposite reaction."
—Sir Isaac Newton

While in school, most of you became familiar with Newton's Third Law—and most of you likely resented it because you were sure you would never have use for something so arcane in the outside world. But as demonstrated by American *kenpo* karate founder Ed Parker, principles of motion are just as important in a *dojo* (karate school) as in a physics class. And because your life may one day depend on your knowledge of motion, it makes sense to have a thorough understanding of this intriguing process.

In the martial arts, however, many systems still work largely on the principle of opposites—right, left, right, left—while ignoring the reverse motion to these movements. Such styles tend to concentrate solely on generating punching power from one side while neglecting to consider the chambered arm as a weapon.

What exactly is meant, then, by the term "reverse motion"? Reverse motion is simply the other half of motion. If, for example, you are driving your car and you shift into reverse, the car starts going backward—the reverse of forward motion. The same concept can be applied to punching motion. When you punch, you perform only the first half of the movement. In order to complete the movement, the striking hand must be retrieved. In doing so, however, it must follow the same path; otherwise it is simply "return motion."

Return motion and reverse motion are also frequently confused, but there is a crucial difference between them. In reverse motion, the hand or foot retraces its movement, following the original axis to its point of origin. Return motion does not necessarily have to follow the same path of action. If, for example, you were to deliver a straight punch and then immediately re-chamber your hand, that would be defined as reverse motion. If, however, you executed an inward block, which immediately converted to a finger strike to the neck and then became a claw strike to your opponent's face before returning to your side, that would be an example of return motion.

Many karate students are trained to attack with a single, devastating

In the example of reverse motion, *kenpo* karate stylist Jesus Flores (right) of Oxnard, California, stops an incoming punch from his brother by using a vertical outward block (1). By reversing the block, Flores can deliver (2) a hammerfist to his brother's head. Continuing to reverse his motion, Flores' original outward block becomes an inward block (3) to stop a second punch.

strike and withdraw, the encounter presumably over. As a student advances through the kenpo system, however, he learns to hit his opponent on the way in and on the way out—a simple form of insurance facilitated by reverse motion. If, for instance, the kenpo practitioner performs an outward block and then reverses its path, with little effort, it can become a hammerfist strike to the opponent's face. If the kenpo stylist advances with an inward elbow strike and, instead of re-chambering the arm in the most direct

By using reverse motion, you can turn your defense into offensive action. In this sequence, *kenpo* stylist Jesus Flores (right) responds (1) to his brother's stick strike with an upward block that becomes an uppercut (2) to the chin, then a forearm strike (3) to the throat. As his brother attempts a punch, Flores reverses the motion of his upward block, resulting in a downward elbow strike (4) to the arm, and continuing into a backward elbow strike (5) to a second attacker's chest.

manner, retraces the strike's path, he can easily deliver an outward elbow smash to the opposite side of his foe's face.

Kenpo practitioners believe that every defense contains an offense, and they are taught to dissect each defensive move in search of offensive potential. They learn that an upward block converts to an uppercut as it rises up the body's centerline, and as the arm begins to rotate, it becomes a rising forearm strike. The reverse motion of this block can result in a vertical back-knuckle strike, a downward elbow smash and, as you chamber the arm, a back elbow strike. There is no wasted motion; you take advantage of the complete movement, not simply the first half of the movement. This is part of the economy of motion that allows kenpo stylists to deliver so many successive strikes in so little time.

Martial artists often squander the versatility provided by reverse motion. People tend to focus only on forward motion—kinetic energy projected away from themselves—and consider the recovery of that motion a dangerous chore to be completed as quickly as possible rather than an opportunity for enhanced action.

Reverse motion can also be used defensively, as illustrated by the "double factor," in which opposite and reverse work together. Say you throw a right outward block and then retrace its path as you throw a left outward block. As the right-hand block reverses itself, it becomes an inward block, providing an interim defense until the left outward block has progressed far enough to be effective.

Increased speed is another benefit of reverse motion. If you have stopped a left-hand punch with an outward block and your opponent throws a right-hand punch, why yank your hand back to your side and throw another block? It is far faster to turn the outward block into an inward block by retracing its course rather than activating your opposite hand, which, if chambered, is much farther away. If a hand is already in the area, why not use it?

The concept of reverse motion can also be applied to forms. People talk occasionally of "hidden" moves in karate *kata* (choreographed training sequences), which suggests that students are performing at least part of their forms without knowing the purpose of the movements. The students would therefore be unable to fully apply the moves unless their instructor reveals the encrypted techniques. This is like giving someone a jigsaw puzzle to work on but withholding key pieces. But because Parker created such an extensive body of martial arts literature, the principles of kenpo are fully defined, and thus constant. Once students grasp the concepts, they can extract the so-called hidden moves themselves because they have been trained to think analytically about motion.

In addition to the practical benefits of reverse motion in a street encounter, instructors may find it a valuable teaching aid. The first kata taught in kenpo is essentially a form done in reverse because the student is moving backward throughout while learning to retreat. This presupposes that you have room to take a step back, an assumption made in many self-defense techniques. But you may find retreat impractical because of an obstacle or an enemy. So when students perform the kata in reverse, they actually move forward and discover that reverse motion can train you to advance as well as withdraw. Accustoming yourself to the instant reversal of motion in a self-defense technique allows you to more easily adapt to circumstances that do not duplicate the ideal conditions under which you learned the maneuver.

Reverse motion can also help demystify certain intimidating movements. When first confronted with executing a spinning kick, for example, some students experience difficulty grasping the mechanics of the technique. If, however, they first perform a familiar move—say a back kick followed by a step forward—then reverse the motion (a back kick and a step back), they suddenly realize that the spinning kick is already in their repertoire.

It should be noted that the principle of reverse motion can also be applied to the use of classical karate weapons such as the *tonfa* (side-handle baton), which is employed today by law-enforcement personnel.

It is also wise to remember that your opponent can utilize reverse motion as well—sometimes unintentionally. If you understand this possibility exists, you are better able to protect yourself against attack or an inadvertent bodily reaction.

Remember that the pain you cause can create an equal and opposite response. But if you learn to properly apply reverse motion, it will more likely be your opponent who demonstrates Newton's First Law: A body at rest tends to remain at rest.

SHOTOKAN KARATE'S SIMULTANEOUS BLOCK
Why Waste Time Waiting to Counterattack?

by Chuck R. Taylor • Photos by Chuck R. Taylor • December 1993

It has been said that, in the "language of karate," basic techniques (*kihon*) such as punches, strikes, blocks and kicks are the individual "letters." And just as combinations of letters form words, combinations of basics form self-defense techniques. Words are subsequently combined to form sentences and paragraphs, in the same way that groups of basic self-defense combinations are linked to become the *kata* (solo training sequences) of karate. In this analogy, basic or prearranged sparring (*sanbon kumite*) is like a scripted conversation. One-step sparring (*ippon kumite*), in which the attack and defense are predetermined, is like a question/answer session, in which each person knows his role. Sparring (*jiyu kumite*) is similar to a free-flowing conversation or debate between two individuals.

Other similarities can be drawn between language and karate. Just as sentences can be simple or complex, so too can karate combinations range from simple block-then-punch sequences to more complex maneuvers, such as a block followed by multiple strikes and kicks to nerve centers, and concluding with a joint lock and takedown. This type of rapid-fire combination is the lifeblood of most modern self-defense systems.

Shotokan karate's simultaneous block/strike is much quicker and more efficient than the traditional block-then-counter method of defending against a punch.

The fifth *heian kata* also includes a simultaneous block/strike—a sweeping left-handed block and right spearhand strike (1 and 2). The maneuver can be used (1a) to thwart an opponent's high punch while countering with a spearhand strike to the groin (2a).

One type of advanced self-defense combination is the simultaneous block/counterattack. In this combination, the opponent attacks and the defender blocks as he simultaneously launches a counterattack. The simultaneous block/counter possesses much more economy of movement than the basic block-then-counter maneuver. To properly execute the more difficult simultaneous block/counter combination, however, you must be able to identify the opponent's initial attack at a very early stage. You have about half the time to perform a simultaneous block/counter as you have to execute a block-then-counter combination. Also, because less body torque is involved in the simultaneous version, the power of your counterattack may be reduced. On the positive side, however, if properly timed and executed, the simultaneous block/counter is so effective that the opponent is generally taken by surprise and literally won't know what hit him.

Some people mistakenly believe that the simultaneous block/strike is the sole territory of Chinese martial arts such as *wing chun*. These same individuals think the Japanese arts, particularly *shotokan* karate, rely on cumbersome and inefficient swinging blocks followed by a lumbering, stiff-armed stepping punch. Both of these beliefs are unfounded. Gichin Funakoshi, shotokan's creator and the man responsible for introducing karate to mainland Japan in 1922, developed a balanced and diverse fighting art by synthesizing many of the best features of the Okinawan and Chinese combat systems. Among Funakoshi's improvisations was the highly effective simultaneous block/counterattack.

Although the simultaneous block/strike is an advanced concept in some self-defense systems, shotokan students are introduced to this combination at a relatively early stage of training. Within the first few months of training, shotokan students begin learning the five *heian* (also known as *pinan*) kata. Although the heian kata are considered somewhat elementary, all but one of these forms contain examples of the simultaneous block/ counterattack.

In the second heian kata, for example, there is a sequence in which the attacker punches to the face with his right hand, and the defender diverts the punch by sweeping it away with his left forearm while countering under the blocking arm with a right palm-up punch (*ura zuki*) to the ribs.

The third heian kata also includes a simultaneous block/strike. In this case, as the attacker punches to the stomach with his right fist, the defender deflects the blow by pushing down on the back of the wrist with his left palm. The defender simultaneously counterattacks over the blocking arm with a right spearhand (*nukite*) to the solar plexus.

The fourth heian form includes a simultaneous block/counter to an attack to the head. As the opponent punches toward the head, the defender redirects the blow with a left openhanded rising block (*shuto age uke*) while simultaneously countering from the side with a knifehand strike (*shuto uchi*) to the jaw.

In the fifth heian kata, there is a segment in which the defender sweeps a chin-high punch to the side with his left palm while simultaneously counterattacking under the blocking arm with a spearhand or palm-heel strike (*teisho*) to the groin.

Shotokan karate's advanced *sochin* form includes three consecutive simultaneous block/strikes (1-3). They are used to block an opponent's midlevel punch while countering with a spearhand to the throat (1a), then block a second midlevel punch while delivering a midlevel front kick (2a) and, finally, to block a face-level punch and counter with a backfist to the face (3a).

All of these simultaneous block/strike combinations are systematic in their approach to defending against an attack. The student learns to counterattack over, under and around his own blocking arm. This helps verify the fact that, while traditional karate kata are not a haphazard series of block-and-counter techniques, they are instead meticulously constructed to lead students from basic to advanced skills.

Another point to keep in mind is that the application or interpretation (*bunkai*) of the moves in each kata can vary from instructor to instructor. For example, the previously discussed block/counter segment from the fourth heian form could be interpreted in a somewhat different manner. Instead of using a knifehand to counter the attacker's head-level punch, the defender could easily substitute a palm-heel strike to the jaw while catching his opponent's right arm. The defender can then push against the opponent's jaw with his palm heel as he pivots to the left, drops to one knee and throws the attacker down.

Although the heian kata feature solid self-defense techniques, they are still rather simple as combinations go. More technically advanced simultaneous block/counter techniques are revealed in intermediate shotokan forms such as jion, an old kata that can be traced to China. Jion contains back-to-back examples of simultaneous block/counter techniques. In the first example, the defender blocks a right-handed punch to the head with his left forearm while countering with a right backfist (*riken*) to the nose. Then, as the attacker follows up with a left-handed punch to the head, the defender deflects the blow by drawing his right forearm back toward his right ear and simultaneously counterattacks with a left-handed punch to the abdomen.

The advanced shotokan kata *sochin* contains a brilliant set of three consecutive simultaneous block/counter combinations. The series begins with the defender deflecting a punch to the midsection by pressing down with his left palm while countering to the opponent's throat with a palm-up spearhand. The defender meets a second punch to the midsection with a simultaneous block/front kick counterattack to the opponent's abdomen. When the attacker follows up with a punch to the chin, the defender parries the blow with the back of his left forearm while simultaneously delivering a right-handed punch to the opponent's upper lip.

*   *   *

The simultaneous block/counter technique is an integral part of shotokan karate, from the beginning level to the advanced stages of black-belt training. The simultaneous combinations are introduced in the kata and are then polished during one-step sparring drills. Although these techniques are a specialty of Japanese karate in general, and shotokan in particular, they continue to remain a virtual secret to those outside the classical Japanese martial arts community.

KENPO'S SPEED HITTING
Is It Necessary, or Is It Overkill?

by Bob Anderson • Photos by Rick Calli • January 1994

The *kenpo* karate instructor stood in a relaxed, natural position, his thumbs resting on the front of his belt. As his student delivered a right-handed punch, however, the instructor underwent a sudden metamorphosis. He swiftly redirected the blow and then exploded in a fury of controlled strikes, delivered from seemingly every angle, striking virtually every conceivable target. The student never had a chance. He was a victim of kenpo's speed-hitting drill.

One of kenpo's most notable characteristics is its emphasis on hitting an opponent numerous times. Some call it overkill; kenpo stylists prefer to call it business as usual. The speed-hitting drill teaches kenpo students how to strike an opponent 10 to 25 times within seconds. The drill bolsters not only self-defense skills, but it also can be applied to forms and sparring practice.

The philosophy behind kenpo's speed training is that, while a worthy opponent may block your first two or three strikes, if you keep hitting him, one of the strikes will reach its target. Speed training teaches you to react quickly and intelligently to your opponent's movements without hesitation.

To practice the speed-hitting drill, round up two partners, one to serve as an attacker and one to time your movements. If a timekeeper is unavailable, the person attacking can hold the stopwatch. Next, set up prearranged sets of techniques with the attacker consisting of 10 to 20 hits apiece. Time your techniques from the first moment of contact to the final moment of contact. This way, you aren't penalized if your partner is a little slow at throwing a punch. Try to maintain eye contact with your opponent's centerline, and use your peripheral vision to spot other open targets. If you videotape your speed-drill techniques, you can watch yourself in motion and look for ways to improve. Recording your hitting speed on a marking board is also useful for tracking your performance.

The following elements are essential in developing rapid striking skills: continuous motion, economy of motion, eliminating wasted motion, timing, compound moves and the concept of relaxing/tensing.

"Continuous motion" is just that—delivering nonstop strikes without hesitation. Your blows should be fluid and continuous, allowing you to build momentum so you are not simply trading punches with your opponent.

Your movements should also possess economy of motion, meaning they should take the most efficient path possible. Just as you would take the quickest and most fuel-efficient route to work, so too should your self-defense strikes take the most economical avenue to the opponent.

The speed of your techniques will increase if you eliminate wasted motion—any unnecessary, time-consuming movement. For example, there is generally no need to first cock your arm before striking or blocking. Eliminate excessive footwork, and be careful not to overextend your movements. Remember that the shortest distance between two points is a straight line. Executing your techniques directly from their point of origin will increase speed and reduce telegraphed movements.

"Timing" suggests synchronizing your strikes with your opponent's movements to obtain maximum results. If you deliver a downward, outward hammerfist to your opponent's groin and immediately follow up with an upward elbow to his chin as he doubles over in response to the groin strike, the result will be much more devastating than if you struck his groin, then cocked your arm and delivered an elbow smash after the opponent had already doubled over.

When practicing basic techniques, students generally execute each block, punch or kick with a singular purpose in mind. However, you can increase the effectiveness of your techniques by adding to them and performing compound moves. For instance, if you are executing a right outward block inside your opponent's left punch, you can extend your right fingers horizontally to rake your opponent's eyes as you perform the block. The same compound move can be applied when performing a right

In this example of *kenpo* karate's speed-hitting drill, the defender (left) faces off (1) with an opponent who delivers a right-handed punch. The defender responds with a double vertical block (2) that transitions into a chop (3) to the neck.

Sequence continued on next page

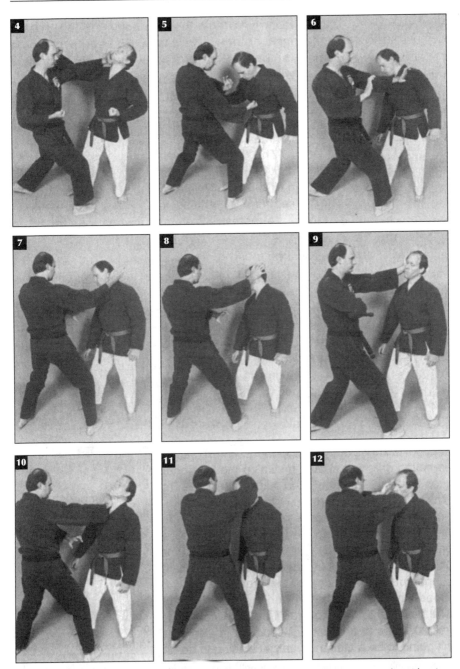

The defender pivots and delivers a palm heel (4) to the chin, followed by an uppercut (5) to the midsection. The defender checks (6) his opponent's shoulder, then unleashes a chop (7) to the neck, right palm heel (8) to the jaw, left palm heel (9) to the jaw and chop (10) to the throat. The defender moves in and executes a simultaneous left palm heel/right elbow smash (11), sandwiching his foe's head. The defender's right elbow slides off and strikes (12) the jaw while his left hand delivers a finger rake across the opponent's face.

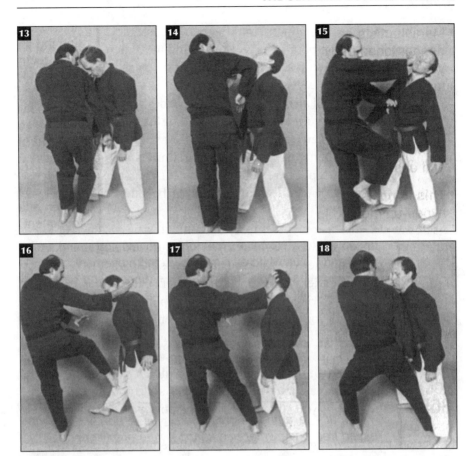

The defender's right hand flows into a hammerfist (13) to the groin and then quickly retracts into an elbow smash (14) to the chin. The defender pivots forward and uncorks (15) a simultaneous knee to the groin and palm heel to the jaw, followed (16) by a simultaneous knifehand to the neck and kick to the knee. The knifehand transitions into a claw (17) to the face, then the defender steps in and delivers (18) a simultaneous hammerfist to the groin and face slap. The defender carefully backs away (19) from his stunned opponent, ending the drill.

inward block inside an opponent's right punch. A basic block has now been transformed into a compound move. Compound movements allow you to execute combinations more rapidly by blending several techniques into one smooth motion.

Your movements will also be quicker if your body is relaxed before and during the execution of your technique. Only at the last moment, just before contact with the opponent, should your block or strike tense up to allow maximum power. It then quickly relaxes again immediately following the strike. This is the concept of "relaxing/tensing." If your muscles are tense during the delivery of a strike, your movement becomes rigid and loses both speed and power.

The amount of tension you employ on contact varies according to the situation. For example, when delivering a right outward knifehand to the right side of your opponent's neck, you can use a small amount of tension to simply jolt him and then follow up with another strike, or you can apply enough tension to the strike to knock out your opponent. When practicing the speed-hitting drill, you should minimize the tension in your techniques to maximize speed and fluidity of movement, and to keep from injuring your partner.

Speed combined with mass creates power, which is why kenpo stylists incorporate their body mass into their strikes. This is accomplished primarily by torquing the body as you strike. The twisting power produced by torque is especially effective for uppercuts, knifehands and forearm strikes.

Kenpo's speed hitting may be viewed by some martial artists as mere "flash"; after all, the likelihood of being able to hit an attacker 20 times in a couple of seconds is slim. The opponent isn't going to be a stationary target waiting to be hit; he is going to be moving and trying to hit you. Even so, the speed drill is an excellent method for developing timing, quickness and focus while eliminating wasted movement.

It would be simple for a marathon runner, who has conditioned himself to run 26 miles, to run a half mile. Likewise, if you condition yourself to perform long, fast techniques, it should be easier and quicker to execute your regular techniques. Therefore, the value of kenpo's speed drill is obvious. It can make any martial artist a better fighter, whether he trains in kenpo or not.

SPECIAL FIGHTING TECHNIQUES OF TANG SOO DO
Add the "Plier Hand," Reverse Chop and Short Spinning Back Kick to Your Combat Arsenal

by Richard Byrne • Photos by Richard Byrne • June 1994

Many martial artists enjoy seeing the techniques that styles other than their own have to offer, even if they never adopt the techniques themselves. The problem is that the only exposure martial artists generally get to other styles is at tournaments, during which competitors are restricted to using only techniques allowed under the rules. Because the rules forbid a wide range of techniques, most styles tend to look very similar in sparring competition. Techniques such as grabs, joint locks and open-hand strikes to the face are all illegal in sparring competition. Although a variety of techniques can be seen during forms competition, one never gets to see these maneuvers practically applied against a real opponent. And many times, the forms' techniques are executed with such quick movements and combinations, it's hard to discern their actual application.

This brings us to three *tang soo do* techniques which, while rarely seen at tournaments, are a welcome addition to any martial artist's fighting arsenal: the "plier hand," the reverse chop and the short spinning back kick.

The "Plier Hand"

The "plier hand" technique can be used as a strike, block or a block that transitions into a grab. The hand is held open, and the fingers and thumb are curved into a "C" shape. The striking surface is the point at which the index finger meets the hand on the palm side. The last two fingers should be used only to reinforce the first two. At no time should the fingers ever spread apart in the plier hand. A sprained or broken finger may result from not keeping the fingers firmly together.

The plier hand can be employed in the same manner you would throw a punch. The targets are primarily restricted to the opponent's larynx and esophagus. A well-placed plier hand can be lethal, preventing the opponent from inhaling properly.

A plier-hand strike can be followed up with a grab by driving the fingers and thumb behind the opponent's larynx and either squeezing or pulling to ensure effective results. This is a potentially deadly application of the plier-hand technique and should be utilized only in life-threatening situations. The plier hand can also be targeted to an opponent's joints, such as the elbow.

There are a number of ways to utilize the plier hand as a blocking technique, but it is most commonly employed in conjunction with a grab. It is an especially effective maneuver against an opponent who is sweating, allowing you to better maintain your grip because of the technique's "C" configuration. Think of your hand as a handcuff or vise, and after blocking your adversary's strike with a plier hand, close your hand around his wrist and lock your grip into place. You will find that the plier-hand technique is

Even though it is an open-hand technique, *tang soo do's* reverse chop is allowed in most tournament sparring competitions. Richard Byrne (left) demonstrates, squaring off (1) with an opponent who throws a punch. Byrne sidesteps and deflects (2) the blow, then unleashes (3) a reverse chop to his opponent's solar plexus.

effective in this manner, even if both you and your opponent are sweating or have oil on your skin.

The Reverse Chop

The reason open-hand techniques are illegal at most martial arts tournaments is to prevent eye injuries. However, although the reverse chop is an open-hand strike, it can be used legally—and effectively—at tournaments.

Two areas of the hand can serve as the striking surface for the reverse chop. The first and most common striking surface is the inside of the first knuckle, where the index finger meets the hand on the inside. This part of the hand is generally used for reverse chops to the opponent's head and body. It's an excellent technique when attempting to fit the strike into tight vital areas such as your adversary's groin or under his nose. The second striking surface for a reverse chop is the area where your index finger and thumb meet. If you look at these two fingers, you will notice they "V" into another bone almost like an oversize knuckle, just in front of where you would wear a watch. If you deliver a reverse chop with this part of the hand, you can deliver a stronger blow with very little risk of injury. Because the fingers are located well away from this area, the chance of hitting them accidentally during the strike is greatly reduced. This part of the hand is very difficult to squeeze into the tight areas, however, and should be delivered to easily accessible targets. The target area and the amount of damage you wish to inflict determines which of the two reverse chops you employ.

To help avoid injury, there are several points to remember when utilizing a reverse chop. First, always keep your fingers firmly together during the strike. Allowing them to separate greatly increases your chance of injury to the fingers. Second, keep your thumb out of the way by bending it in against your palm. The thumb is quite useless in this technique and only gets in the way. You will have to make a conscious effort to keep the thumb in a safe position to avoid injury.

You might ask, "Why not simply throw a punch instead of a reverse chop so you don't have to worry about protecting your fingers and thumb?"

Although it might be easier to throw a punch, there are several instances in which the reverse chop has an advantage over a straight punch. The reverse chop is most commonly used like a boxer's hook punch. This gives the martial artist an effective strike even in close quarters, where a straight punch simply will not work well. Moreover, how would you defend yourself if the last two fingers on your hand were sprained or broken? A punch is totally out of the question in this case because you cannot make a fist. Even a traditional chopping technique might not be appropriate because you may hit your injured little finger. Obviously, a reverse chop makes complete sense in this case because you can strike your opponent without damaging your injured hand. A reverse chop can be delivered in two ways: the "windmill" method and the hook. In the windmill delivery, the arm is extended as far from your target as possible and is whipped in a circular motion toward the opponent. The hook method allows you to extend your arm and whip the reverse chop at a slight angle from your target. Tournament competitors commonly use the hook version of the reverse chop because it is quicker and more deceptive than the windmill method. You should never fully lock your arm on either reverse chop delivery. You can extend your arm, but maintain a slight bend to prevent hyperextension of the elbow.

A strong reverse chop should snap out toward the target. Just as you would twist a traditional reverse punch, you need to "load" the reverse chop in the opposite position and snap it over approximately six to eight inches before striking your target. The snapping motion increases the technique's velocity and power.

Short Spinning Back Kick

Martial arts that stress kicking over hand techniques, such as tang soo do and *taekwondo*, are often criticized because their kicks require ample distance from the target to be executed effectively. This is why tang soo

Richard Byrne (left) faces off (1) with an opponent to demonstrate how *tang soo do's* reverse chop can be applied in a self-defense situation. As the opponent punches, Byrne sidesteps (2).

do includes in its arsenal the short spinning back kick, which allows you to throw a powerful kick at close range.

The short spinning back kick is employed primarily when your opponent is in a side stance and offers no open straight-line targets. The striking surface for the kick is the bottom of your heel. The kick is extremely powerful. Even if your opponent attempts to block the technique with his arms or shoulders, it can cause damage.

The short spinning back kick is executed in the same manner as a regular spinning back kick. It is a rear-leg kick, meaning it has more power, which is generated by the spinning motion of your body.

When you turn to start the kick, your rear leg should come up immediately. It helps to pretend that there is a piano bench behind you, so as you begin the kick, you must lift your rear leg immediately to avoid hitting the bench. The reason for lifting the leg so soon is twofold. First, it enhances the kick's velocity. And second, if your opponent lifts his knee to block or jam your kick, your rear leg will pass right over his front leg, making your kick next to impossible to stop.

The short spinning back kick must be employed at close range to be effective. The technique serves as an excellent counterattack against an opponent's skipping roundhouse kick or any time your adversary overextends his kick. The kick is also effective when delivered after you have set up your opponent with several hand techniques.

He blocks the punch downward (3) and delivers (4) a reverse chop to the area under the aggressor's nose.

One danger when employing the short spinning back kick occurs when your opponent manages to shift out of the way of the technique, putting him in a good position to counterattack. If you fail to finish the kick and return to your starting position, the front of your body is vulnerable and begging to be hit. If, however, you complete the circular motion of the kick, you will return to a fighting stance, prepared to defend yourself.

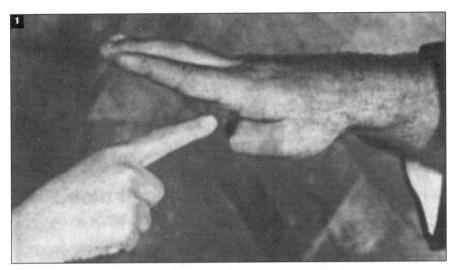

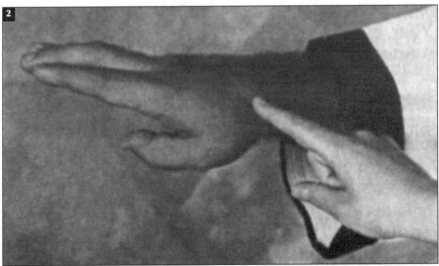

The reverse chop can be delivered in one of two ways. You can strike with the area where the index finger meets the hand (1), delivering a chop to the opponent's head or body. Or when striking more inaccessible targets, such as the groin or under the nose, you can use the area where your index finger and thumb meet (2).

BRUCE LEE'S FAVORITE FIGHTING TECHNIQUE
The "Dragon" Felt the Forward Hand Strike Was the Most Efficient Way to Defeat an Opponent

by Robert W. Young and Jerry Beasley, Ed.D. • *Photos by Carey Frame* • *July 1994*

In his book *Tao of Jeet Kune Do*, Bruce Lee outlined the requirements for incorporating a technique into one's personal fighting style. To be useful, he claimed, a technique must be nontelegraphic, initiated from a mobile stance, delivered at the correct moment and compatible with efficient follow-up maneuvers. Lee also discussed in his text training methods, mobility concepts, distance-controlling techniques and philosophical principles, all of which relate to the original theme of being simple and direct in fighting. The concept of fighting with your strong side forward offers further proof that Lee's entire combat method stressed simplicity. "The first principle for fastest contact in attacking from a distance is using the longest [weapon] to get at the closest [target]," Lee wrote.

Former full-contact karate champion and *Black Belt* Hall of Fame member Joe Lewis recalls that, during his two years of apprenticeship under Lee, these principles were paramount. Lee always stressed the importance of mastering a few good techniques. As a result, Lewis compiled an incredible tournament sparring record using just two primary weapons: the front-leg side kick and the forward hand strike.

It took Lewis, Lee's premier fighting student, 14 months of daily four-hour workouts to master these two skills. Although Lee, an extremely quick and dynamic martial artist, perfected the *jeet kune do* system, Lewis attributes its popularity to something else. "Explosiveness makes JKD what it is today," Lewis says. Consequently, a quick fighter can make better use of the system's principles than a powerful fighter.

Lee said, "The leading straight punch is the backbone of all punching in jeet kune do. Most experts make [it] their principal blow."

Following is Lewis' interpretation of jeet kune do's forward hand strike and his unique method for teaching it.

Stance and Footwork

Lee determined that a correct on-guard position should feature a slightly bent knee because it facilitates freedom of movement. Lewis agrees with Lee and considers footwork the premier mechanical aspect of jeet kune do. Therefore, to properly perform the forward hand strike, a martial artist must adjust his stance to approximate Lee's fighting posture. Lewis claims that Lee melded the classic *wing chun* kung fu stance with a fencer's stance

Notice the differences between the *jeet kune do* fighter's stance (1, left) and the stance of the traditional karate stylist (1, right). The JKD fighter's feet are closer together and his hands are higher to protect his head. The JKD stance (2, left) is somewhat similar to a kickboxing stance (2, right).

and that he paid little attention to the traditional boxing stance because he wanted to make his initial move more explosive.

The toes of the front foot should point toward the opponent or slightly to the side so the front leg can attack quickly. From this position, the JKD stylist's front leg can trap the opponent's front leg or prevent him from advancing, thus siphoning power from the opponent's lead-leg or lead-hand techniques.

Jeet kune do students are taught to place their strong side forward to rapidly penetrate their opponent's defensive perimeter with a technique such as the forward hand strike. In this stance, the front hand becomes the primary weapon, while the rear hand remains a viable backup for defense or a follow-up strike.

Both hands remain high to protect the centerline, including the defender's face and solar plexus. Unlike Thai boxers, who often bait their opponents into attacking their midsection, JKD stylists keep their elbows close to their body to defend their ribs and abdomen.

Lewis emphasizes that students must explode toward their opponent. Anyone who has watched Lewis or Lee in action can attest to their ability to quickly cover great distances to strike their opponents. Unlike fencers, who also explode forward quickly, JKD stylists have the added advantage of lateral mobility.

Jeet kune do fighters use explosive footwork to penetrate an opponent's perimeter and disrupt his balance. Once the opponent is forced to shift his weight onto his heels, Lewis claims, "he is defensively helpless and offensively handcuffed." The same thing occurs when an opponent straightens his knees in response to a JKD fighter's oncoming forward hand strike.

Offensive Principles

Lee wrote, "Relaxation is essential for faster and more powerful punching." Relaxing before delivering an explosive punch is the secret to generating maximum speed during jeet kune do's forward hand strike. "You have to translate the mental concept of exploding into a physical attribute," Lewis advises. "The 'trigger squeeze' is all-important."

"Trigger squeeze" refers to a technique's "initial" speed, which is the most significant of the three kinds of speed Lewis identifies. Initial speed comes into play while the hand moves from its initial position to about halfway to the target. It gives the attacking limb momentum—the key to

A comparison of the finish of a *jeet kune do* punch (1) and a boxer's jab (2). Notice how the JKD stylist places the weight on his front foot for added power and also turns his front foot slightly. The boxer, meanwhile, has his weight on his rear foot and his front foot is pointed toward his opponent.

power. Initial speed is equally important for effective footwork.

Second in importance is "miles per hour" speed, the rate at which a limb travels to the target or point of interception. The key to this type of speed lies in being relaxed and having strong muscles. Miles-per-hour speed can often be controlled or enhanced by deception.

Lewis describes timing as the third component of speed development. "Timing is best when the opponent rushes in," Lee wrote. Timing is the correct measure for explosive penetration.

"During the forward hand strike, don't jerk the hand back," Lewis advises. "Let the natural elasticity of the muscles retract the arm."

A bent elbow at the end of the forward hand strike indicates a lack of power. "You are smothering your own punch, which makes it easier for your opponent to move inside your defenses," Lee said, always reminding students to straighten out their punches. Power for the forward hand strike comes in the last three inches of the technique. "Punch through the opponent, instead of at him," Lee advised.

A common mistake is to not keep the shoulders level during the forward hand strike. Avoid teetering or swaying, Lewis cautions. "When your shoulders aren't level, you're off-balance," he notes. "When you're off-balance, you lose speed. When you lose speed, you lose power. When you lose power, not only do you not win, you run out of gas."

Five Elements of the Forward Hand Strike

Lewis divides the forward hand strike into five sequential parts. The first part dictates that the striking limb always moves first. When a JKD stylist begins the strike, his fist practically falls from its high on-guard position, down and out toward the target.

The second segment teaches students to keep their elbow centered. Allowing the elbow to stray outward decreases punching power. Lee wrote that the elbow should serve as protection against counterattacks and provide a strategic position for follow-up strikes.

The third part of Lewis' equation notes that torque comes from twisting the shoulder and hip. During the forward hand strike, these twists may seem small, but the length of the arm amplifies both speed and power. Arm muscles help when punching, but the power they impart cannot match that generated by the twisting motion of the shoulder and hip. Lee wrote, "Power in hitting comes from a quick twist of the waist, not a swinging, swaying movement, but a pivot over the straight lead leg."

The fourth aspect of the forward hand strike involves shifting your body weight onto your front foot. Lewis says that the front leg should support 60 percent to 70 percent of your weight and that the knee should straighten out for maximum power. Do not imitate boxers, who place 60 percent of their weight on the rear foot and bend the front knee after jabbing.

The fifth part of the technique is the forward step, usually about six to eight inches to start. Never drag the rear foot, which Lewis claims causes a loss of speed because the fighter cannot derive the essential power from his hip. "It's like putting out an anchor," Lewis says.

While it is important to keep these elements in mind, you should concentrate on making your fist move first, Lewis says. "Let the footwork and shoulder movement take care of themselves," he states. Lewis insists the

Bruce Lee often preferred to deliver the forward hand strike after first setting up his opponent. In this example, Joe Lewis (right) squares off (1) with an opponent and fakes (2) as if he is about to raise his front leg for a side kick. The opponent reacts to the fake, dropping his hands, leaving him vulnerable to Lewis' forward hand strike (3) to the head.

weight of a fist is sufficient to knock out an opponent; therefore, a fighter should focus on moving it quickly and correctly.

Practicing the Forward Hand Strike

To improve your forward hand strike, you must perform a variety of drills. A full-length mirror can greatly aid your training by allowing you to watch for mistakes. Coordination and mobility drills will allow you to implement the principles of the strike. For best results, perform drills with a partner and without additional equipment. During this training phase, balance, speed, timing and distancing are practiced and honed.

Finally, application and strategy drills are performed. The student and his partner can practice one aspect of strategy at a time during sparring sessions, or they can free spar and utilize all their knowledge and techniques together. "It is only during the application drills that one can achieve confidence and real self-assurance in the execution of the forward hand strike," Lewis notes.

Lewis advises students not to limit their use of the forward hand strike principles only to hitting opponents. With minor modifications, the principles can easily be used to fake, immobilize an opponent's limb or set up an opponent for a different technique. Additionally, the principles of the forward hand strike can apply to JKD's rear hand strike and lead-leg obstructing kick.

When practicing the forward hand strike, be sure to vary the distance between you and your opponent. "If you can tag somebody from the six-foot distance, you know you're firing a perfect JKD forward hand strike," Lewis notes. "And once you get the principles down, it's easy to convert them to rear-hand [techniques], the lead-leg round kick, the lead-leg side kick or the lead-leg obstruction [maneuver]." According to Lewis, these are the best offensive techniques in the JKD arsenal.

WANT TO TRIPLE YOUR HITTING SPEED?
12 Steps to Faster Fighting Techniques
by Steven Barnes • October 1994

Speed. Blinding, numbing, eye-baffling speed is probably the most sought-after and visually impressive skill in the martial arts. Bruce Lee's lightning-fast punches literally made his reputation. Speed is also what distinguishes many of the top professional boxers, such as former champions Sugar Ray Leonard and Muhammad Ali. Ali's power was only adequate for his size, but his hand speed was phenomenal. And Leonard had perhaps the fastest hands the boxing world has ever seen. Likewise, former full-contact karate champion Bill Wallace was never acclaimed for his kicking power but rather for his awesome foot speed, which was largely responsible for his undefeated professional ring record.

Is this illusive physical magic reserved for the genetically gifted few, or can speed really be developed and improved through training? According to Dr. John LaTourrette—a black belt in *kenpo* karate who holds a doctorate degree in sports psychology—anyone can be trained to be a "speed hitter" merely by following a few basic principles.

"Speed training is 90 percent mental—maybe 99 percent," LaTourrette says. This mental training approach to speed seems to have worked for the lanky 50-year-old karate instructor from Medford, Oregon. He has reportedly been clocked at 16.5 hits per second and claims he has students who can hit even faster. The following is his 12-step program to increase speed.

• **Learn by watching the experts.** "If a man wants to be a fast runner, he doesn't go out and study a cripple in a wheelchair," LaTourrette says. "What he needs to do is go out and find a fast runner about his own age, shape and body physiology, and then study how that man moves and do exactly what he does."

• **Use fluid strikes.** Fluid Chinese-style striking techniques are much more explosive than the traditional karate reverse punch or boxing's jabs, LaTourrette claims, because the hitting speed is generated by momentum. You can train your mind and nervous system for speed hitting. To do this, set up a "flow drill"—a sequence of movements, starting with three or four at a time. Once this combination of techniques becomes automatic, add a few more movements and then a few more, until you have trained your subconscious mind to link the individual moves into one overall fluid movement. After a while, the entire 15 or 20 moves can be completed in one second or less.

• **Use focused aggression.** You must be able to instantly shift from a relaxed state to one of combat readiness to attack your opponent before he is aware of your motion. Any doubts about your ability to defend yourself must be eliminated through mental training before you get into an altercation.

There are three facets to reaction time—perception, decision and action—which together take approximately six-tenths of a second to resolve. Perceptions and decisions should be made while in a nonaggressive stance so as not to tip off your opponent. Once you are focused, your attack can be executed before your opponent can blink an eye.

To properly execute this type of attack, you must be absolutely clear of your right and ability to take action, or you will hesitate. As LaTourrette tells his students, "Talking don't cook the rice." You must be aggressive and have confidence in your skill. Your confidence should be based on hands-on training against a live opponent rather than on *kata* practice against an imaginary opponent.

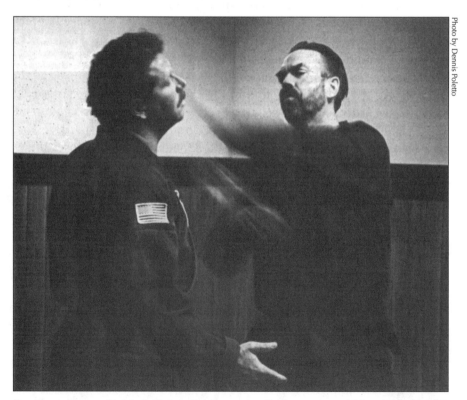

Photo by Dennis Poletto

Kenpo karate instructor Dr. John LaTourrette (right) can reportedly hit an opponent 16 times in one second.

You must be constantly aware, alert to your environment and ready to release a relaxed explosiveness should the need arise. This physical, mental and emotional state can be learned easily and naturally by every student, but only by experiencing real confrontations against a live opponent.

Once you have achieved this state of readiness, analyze it and try to categorize the sensations you feel. Later, in a combat situation, you can draw on these experiences, much as an actor does, and use them to your advantage. Ask yourself the following questions: What specifically triggers my state of focused awareness? Is it the opponent's distance from me? Is it his external signs of aggression? His speech patterns? How did it feel to be in that mental state? What sensations did I experience? What was my posture like? What facial expressions did I make? What muscles were tensed? Which muscles were relaxed? What, if anything, was I saying to myself while in this state? (Ideally, there should be no internal "babble.") Did I visualize any images in my mind? What was I visually focused on?

After answering these questions, imagine yourself back in a state of readiness, intensifying the feelings, pictures and sounds in your mind. Experiment until you can place yourself in this mental state at will.

• **Use a ready stance that gives you a variety of options.** One of the secrets to Wallace's success was that, from a single leg position, he could instantly deliver a side kick, roundhouse kick or hook kick with equal precision. Similarly, your ready stance should be versatile enough to allow you to unleash knifehands, claw-hand strikes, elbow smashes, eye jabs or hammerfists, depending on your opponent's movements.

Practice fighting techniques that feel natural to you. Learn to position yourself so that only a tiny shift is required to move from one target to another. Adopting a natural fighting posture eliminates the need to assume a stance and allows you to catch your opponent off-guard. A confused opponent is an easy opponent—one already half beaten.

• **Avoid the "one-punch kill" mentality.** This is a corollary to rule No. 1. Your initial attack should always be a three-strike sequence, even if your first blow is strong enough to stop a charging opponent. The first strike is the "appetizer," the second is the "main course" and the third is "dessert."

"While your unsuspecting opponent is getting set for a straight punch or rear-leg kick," LaTourrette says, "you can slap a 'blinder' into his eyes, a left fist to his temple and a right elbow to his other temple. Then you can rake your right elbow across his jaw as you rake his eyes with your left hand. Drop into a kneeling stance and follow up with a right hammerfist to the groin and a left-hand two-finger eye jab to his head. End of story."

• **Use visualization drills.** When practicing speed-hitting drills, you must be able to see yourself performing the movements at the desired speed. "If you can't see it, you can't do it," LaTourrette says. Such mental training actually aids your physical skills.

Visualization is not as difficult as some people believe. Try this experiment: Stop right now and tell yourself the color of your car. Now describe an orange. Now describe your best friend.

How did you know how to describe these things? You saw them. Many people are not aware that they frequently make "pictures" in their heads on a subconscious level. The part of your mind that creates and recreates images can be fine-tuned, even if you are unaccustomed to tapping into it.

Once you can visualize yourself in a fight scenario just as if you were watching a movie of yourself, practice seeing and feeling your natural weapons ripping through your chosen targets. Feel the bend in your knees add power to your blows. Feel the pressure on the ball of your foot as you push off.

• **Identify open targets.** To learn how to identify open targets and predict your opponent's actions, it is essential to practice with a live partner. This acute sense of timing is achieved by practicing your attacks repeatedly until no conscious thought is involved in the action.

One reason boxers have such good hand speed is that they practice their techniques thousands of times with a sparring partner. When an opening appears, they don't think, they move. This subconscious skill is easy to acquire, but there are no shortcuts. You must put in the training time until your responses are instinctive.

• **Don't "telegraph" your movements.** No matter how quick you are, if your opponent knows what is coming, you are not quick enough. Believe it or not, a strike that comes directly at an opponent at eye level is much harder for him to see than a hook punch that comes from the side. A hook punch contains more motion and is therefore easy to block. Conversely, a properly delivered jab can hit your opponent between the eyes before he knows you have released a punch. Be sure not to telegraph your strike to the opponent by clenching your fist, moving your shoulder or taking a deep breath before you deliver the blow.

Once the basic physical structure of your techniques is drilled to perfection, practice taking advantage of the limitations of human perception by positioning yourself in a way that blocks your opponent's view of your actions. This takes much practice, but once you get the knack of it, you will be able to strike your sparring partners with impunity.

• **Use proper breathing methods.** Many karate practitioners slow themselves down by holding their breath while fighting. This tenses your entire body, impeding your quickness and reducing the force of your strikes. Likewise, unleashing a loud *kiai* before delivering a technique is even worse because it stops your momentum. The key to speed hitting is to expel air in conjunction with your strikes.

• **Maintain a high level of fitness.** General flexibility, strength and endurance are advantageous for self-defense, even though most street fights are over in a matter of seconds. If you are both flexible and relaxed, you can kick instantly from multiple angles, to high or low targets, without awkward stance changes. Leg strength is also vital. The stronger your legs, the harder you can kick and the faster you will move when closing the gap between you and your opponent. It is also important to strengthen your arms and shoulders through weight training and specific striking drills. Exercises can also strengthen your wrists and hands, improving your striking accuracy and penetration.

• **Persevere.** You must make a commitment of 20 to 30 minutes, three times a week, to noticeably improve your hitting speed. Be prepared for the inevitable plateau periods, when you feel you are not making any progress.

Most people experience five levels of progress or plateaus during their training. There is "unconscious incompetence," in which you are unaware of any problems or solutions. "Conscious incompetence" is the point at which you become aware that your knowledge or skills are insufficient, and you take action to remedy the problem. "Conscious competence" means you

Photo from *Black Belt* Archives

Fitness and flexibility are important factors in improving your hitting speed for self-defense.

can perform a new skill, but only if your attention is focused. This is the most difficult stage of training and seems to drag on forever. The process of transforming a conscious thought into reflexive action takes approximately 3,000 to 5,000 repetitions. "Unconscious competence" is the only level at which true speed becomes possible, as you learn to react instinctively. Only thousands of technique repetitions can take you to this level. Most people are in this reflexive or automatic mental state when driving their cars, allowing them to react to traffic hazards with disassociated calm because they are not worried about how to change gears, turn the wheel or hit the brakes. You will not be able to improve your hitting speed until you can perform basic maneuvers reflexively. The final stage of training is "conscious of your unconscious competence," a point few people ever reach.

• **Maintain a natural, relaxed, balanced stance.** The best fighting stances are those which don't look like fighting stances. As legendary Japanese swordsman Musashi Miyamoto put it, "Your combat stance becomes your everyday stance, and your everyday stance becomes your combat stance." You must know exactly what techniques can be thrown from each position and must be able to execute them instantly, without hesitation or shifting stances.

*   *   *

Practice one of these 12 principles for 20 minutes each day. After a month of training, you will develop new and overwhelming speed. As LaTourrette says, "There are no natural speed fighters. Every one of us had to learn the same way. The more you sweat in training, the less you hurt in combat."

HAND STRIKES OF KAJUKENBO
Hit Hard, Hit Fast and Hit Often
by John Bishop • Photos by John Bishop • December 1994

Fierce, brutal, effective—these are just a few of the words used to describe *kajukenbo*, widely considered the first martial art created in the United States. Kajukenbo, a combination of five combat systems, gained its tough reputation decades ago in what was then the U.S. territory of Hawaii, where the style was synthesized. Kajukenbo's no-nonsense approach to self-defense has earned the style recognition worldwide as an efficient and devastating fighting art.

Kajukenbo's Origin

Kajukenbo is a prime example of American ingenuity. It was founded in 1949 in the U.S. territory of Hawaii. According to San Clemente, California-based kajukenbo instructor Gary Forbach, the style was formulated in 1947, when five Hawaiian martial arts teachers, calling themselves the "Black Belt Society," collaborated on a project to develop a comprehensive self-defense system. These five men of vision were Peter Choo, the Hawaiian welterweight boxing champion and a black belt in *tang soo do*; Frank Ordonez, a *sekeino jujutsu* black belt; Joe Hoick, a *kodokan* judo black belt; Clarence Chang, a master of *sil lum pai* kung fu; and Adriano D. Emperado, an *escrima* expert and black belt in Chinese *kenpo*.

The talented quintet trained together several hours each day, sharing the strengths and weaknesses of each other's systems as they created a new and highly comprehensive art. While sparring with Choo, Hoick discovered flaws in some of his striking techniques. Choo, on the other hand, realized his style left him vulnerable once he was on the ground. Emperado demonstrated to Choo how a kenpo stylist could get inside the tang soo do stylist's kicks and deliver rapid-fire hand techniques. Chang showed the others how the circular, flowing techniques of sil lum pai could be used to evade and strike an opponent. And Ordonez demonstrated to his cohorts how a jujutsu practitioner absorbs an attacker's force and redirects it against him in the form of painful locks and throws.

After deciding that kenpo would serve as the foundation from which to build on, the five martial artists began an arduous three-year process of incorporating tang soo do kicks, jujutsu joint locks, judo throws and sil lum pai circular techniques into one fighting system. Eventually, all that was needed was a name for the new style. Hoick suggested that the system

101

be called kajukenbo—*ka* for karate, *ju* for judo and jujutsu, *ken* for kenpo and *bo* for Chinese boxing (kung fu).

Today, kajukenbo is practiced worldwide and is represented by the International Kajukenbo Association, based in Oakland, California.

Gary Forbach (right) faces off (1) with an opponent to demonstrate a *kajukenbo* hand-strike combination. Forbach blocks (2) a punch and counters with a palm heel (3) to the sternum, knuckle punch (4) to the eye, hammerfist (5) to the groin and palm heel (6) to the face. Notice how Forbach selects his strikes according to his opponent's reaction to each blow.

Kajukenbo Hand Strikes

Kajukenbo is noted for its rapid hand combinations and low kicks. The hand strikes evolved from Emperado's vast knowledge of Chinese kenpo and escrima. Emperado also studied thousands of techniques and types of movement from other systems, and he used principles of physics to analyze existing hand techniques and develop more efficient methods of striking. Emperado believed in the tenet that "for every action there is an equal and opposite reaction." When applied to the martial arts, this principle refers to the fact that, when struck, the body will react in a certain manner. Forbach claims this point is especially significant to kajukenbo stylists because they utilize multiple hand strikes in rapid succession. "We have all seen demonstrations by martial artists who have tremendous hand speed," Forbach relates. "Unfortunately, in the case of some, when you break down their strikes, you realize that half of them would not have been effective or even hit their desired targets. Rapidly striking an opponent several times is useless if your strikes do not hit your intended targets."

Before you can begin to improve your hand speed, you must learn how the body reacts to various strikes. If, for example, your first strike was a reverse punch to the opponent's stomach, it would not be effective to target his face with a follow-up backfist strike. If executed properly, the first strike to the stomach should cause the opponent to bend forward. Thus, he would be looking toward the ground and his face would not be at an angle that could be easily targeted with a backfist. A more effective approach would be to reverse the sequence of strikes: Hit the opponent's face with a backfist, causing his head to snap backward, then strike the exposed stomach with a follow-up reverse punch.

According to Forbach, target selection is critical when attempting multiple hand strikes. "This is where you have to have an exceptional understanding of body movement," he notes. "Thankfully, professor Emperado saved kajukenbo stylists thousands of hours of evaluation, analyzation, and trial and error. The system he developed utilizes a myriad of effective self-defense combinations, which are taught progressively to kajukenbo students as they advance through the ranks."

Developing Hand Speed

Hand speed is difficult to improve. Repetition training can increase speed somewhat, but other factors such as "flow" and "economy of motion" can have a greater influence on the speed of your techniques. Because kajukenbo employs both circular and linear hand strikes, it lends itself well to flowing movement.

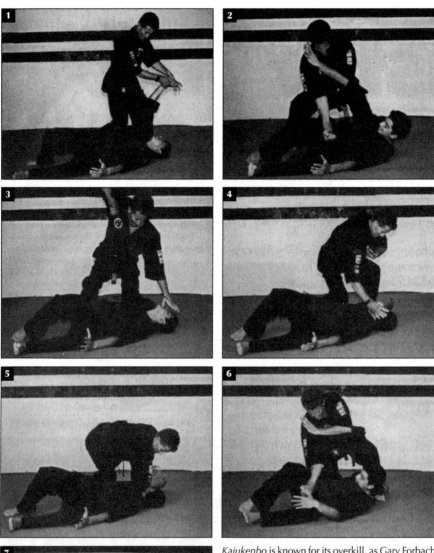

Kajukenbo is known for its overkill, as Gary Forbach demonstrates here. After taking his opponent down (1), Forbach unleashes a series of hand strikes to make sure he stays down, delivering a backfist (2) to the groin, knifehand (3) to the face, palm heel (4) to the jaw, elbow smash (5) to the jaw, a second backfist (6) to the groin and a palm heel (7) to the jaw. End of fight.

Instead of executing separate strikes, the kajukenbo stylist attempts to deliver techniques without pause, each transitioning smoothly into the next. If, for example, you struck an opponent on the side of his neck with a knifehand, rather than retracting the hand, you would redirect the strike straight down to your adversary's groin. The groin strike can then be redirected upward and converted into an uppercut to the face.

By moving in the most economical manner possible—thus reducing the distance your hand must travel to reach its target—you can significantly increase your hand speed. For example, a jab or backfist will reach your opponent more quickly than a reverse punch because the first two techniques begin from a closer position to your adversary. Of course, neither a jab nor backfist pack the power of a reverse punch, so there is a trade-off. Proper body mechanics will help you develop increased power behind these shorter techniques. By torquing the hips and shoulders, you can add momentum as you deliver such strikes. Increased power can also be achieved by dropping your weight into downward strikes and "lifting" with your legs when striking upward.

You should consider both economy and flow when selecting which hand strikes to employ. Circular techniques, such as knifehands, can be quickly converted into snapping maneuvers, like backfists. Open-hand strikes tend to be faster because the arm muscles are more relaxed when the hand is not clenched in a fist. Thrusting techniques, such as your straight punches, are more powerful but slower to redirect. It is therefore wise, when striking multiple times, to hold your thrusting punch in reserve and use it as a finishing technique.

*   *   *

To achieve effective, rapid, multiple hand strikes, whether or not you train in kajukenbo, you must: a) learn how the body reacts when hit; b) understand flow and the use of economical motion; c) understand which techniques work best together; and d) practice the techniques repeatedly to develop your hand speed.

INCREASE YOUR STRIKING POWER!
Understanding Principles of Physics Can Improve Your Hitting Skills

by Scott W. Teare • Photos by D. McQuay • March 1995

Most people remember their high-school physics class as a series of endless equations, taught by an instructor who seemed to go out of his way to make the subject dull. Once they passed the class, they immediately forgot about physics, believing it was insignificant in their everyday lives. Many of these same individuals may be surprised to discover, however, that an understanding of physics can be invaluable to martial arts training, improving both form and power. Maybe *now* you wish you had paid more attention in physics class.

The study of mechanics, particularly kinematics and dynamics, is one of the elements of physics most applicable to the martial arts. Kinematics, which deals with various types of motion, and dynamics, which examines the relation between force and resulting motion, are the principles that govern many striking techniques.

A quiz published in the August 1988 issue of *Black Belt* is testimony to the relation between physics and the martial arts. The quiz contained nine questions that tested the readers' knowledge about how to optimize various techniques. Six of the questions required an understanding of physics to

---

Table 1
EQUATIONS FOR STRIKING

1) $KE = (1/2) mv^2$	a = acceleration
2) $F = ma$	m = mass
3) Total energy in = total energy out	x,v = position, velocity
4) $v^2 = v_0^2 + 2a(x-x_0)$	F = force
5) $dF = dP/dt = d(mv)/dt$	KE = kinetic energy
6) $v = wr$	p = pressure
7) $p = F/S$	P = momentum
	t = time
	w = degrees per second
	r = radius of rotation
	S = surface area

Note: Any variable preceded by "d" represents a change in that variable. The subscript "o" represents the initial condition of the variable.

reach a correct answer. Some of the concepts presented in that quiz will be developed in this article. A group of equations that govern striking are listed in Table 1, along with an explanation of the symbols. Don't be daunted by these equations; a little pencil scratching will make it all clear. The picture can be simplified by considering the striking surface—of the hand, foot, etc.—as a solid entity. Some subtleties are obviously lost in this

Overhead strikes such as this (1-3) are an example of circular motion. The shoulder acts as the pivot or axis of rotation of the striking arc.

interpretation, but the equations address almost every detail of building power and understanding striking.

Begin by considering the speed of the fist just before hitting a target. This speed is about 13.9 meters per second (30 miles per hour). The path of a punch is about one meter (39 inches) from the cocked position to full extension, and the mass of a fist is about .25 kilograms (1/2 pound). With this information and equation 1, we can determine the amount of energy that can be imparted to the target when struck. Remember, mass is not the same as weight. Weight, as measured on a bathroom scale, is the acceleration resulting from gravity acting upon a mass (see equation 2).

It is a known fact that, if you increase the energy imparted to a target, the strike has more effect. What is the best way to increase the energy? If you examine equation 1, you will see there are two variables: mass and velocity. If you double the mass of the fist while maintaining the same fist speed, you will double the energy behind the blow. However, because the velocity is squared in the equation, doubling the fist speed alone will result in a fourfold increase in the energy.

Scribbling down a few lines of math is a small price to pay for understanding the dynamics of fist speed. Regardless of your knowledge, however, a 27-meter-per-second (60 miles per hour) punch is a pipe dream (although former kickboxing champion Bill Wallace is said to have reached 70 miles per hour with some kicks). What you *can* learn from these calculations is that you should always try to reach maximum fist velocity just before striking a target. It should also be noted that the principle of getting one's weight behind a strike has not been factored into the equations. Striking with your entire body increases your striking mass, which in turn provides additional force.

While it is wise to retract your fist after striking to prevent it from being grabbed and to prepare for a follow-up attack, you should avoid snapping the fist back too quickly. The "conservation of energy rule" states that the amount of energy going into an event must be the same as that after the event (see equation 3). The idea in a striking technique is to maximize the energy transferred to the target. If some of the total energy provided by the punch is used in retracting the fist, then, according to the conservation of energy rule, less energy is imparted to the target.

The physics of snapping back a punch focuses on the relation between impulse and force. The force applied to a target is based on the deceleration experienced by the fist on contact with the target. The deceleration is dependent on the distance in which the fist comes to a stop. If you hit a

The circular knifehand strikes (1-2) of karate's *pinan yondan kata* and the *sai* strikes (1a-2a) of the *matsu higa-no-sai* kata illustrate how a weapon can be used to increase the radius of a strike. When both the knifehand and sai move through the same number of degrees of arc, in the same amount of time, the sai strike will impart more energy to the target because of its increased speed. The additional mass of the weapon also increases the energy of the strike.

hard or rigid target, a greater force can be imparted than if you hit a soft target, whereby the fist penetrates deeply into the target. This results from the fist decelerating at a lower rate in the soft target (see equation 4).

The concept of impulse is more difficult to appreciate, but it has to do with the change-in-momentum-per-unit time. Because the mass of the striking implement (that is, a fist) does not change as a function of time and momentum is the mass times the velocity of the fist, then impulse is really just the product of the force and the length of time the force is applied (see equation 5). Thus, impulse is another measure of the momentum. Remember, the key contributor to the amount of force delivered to the target is directly related to the deceleration of the fist in the target.

The same principle of maximizing the velocity, thus leading to greater force and energy, can also be applied to circular movements. The velocity of a circular strike is the distance from the pivot point (radius of rotation) times the number of degrees of arc passed through per unit time (see equation 6). Maximum velocity is therefore reached by maximizing these two values. Once again, maximizing the velocity will maximize the energy of the strike.

A final note: One often hears about the devastating effects of a *wing chun* kung fu punch because of its ability to generate great hydrostatic pressure in the area of impact. How does hydrostatic pressure relate to the preceding discussion of force and energy? Pressure equals the force per unit area (see equation 7). This means that the smaller the area a force acts on, the larger the pressure. This is why the smallest and hardest surfaces of the fist (the first two knuckles) are the usual contact areas of a punch. The wing chun punch also makes use of the impulse concept in that the blow's unique additional flick upward on impact provides an increase in the velocity at the point of contact. Because this type of punch provides greater force with its nonlinear acceleration (in time) over a small surface area (the bottom knuckle), it develops greater pressure changes in the target than a standard karate punch.

*   *   *

As you can see, physics is inherently contained in the martial arts. Assimilating this knowledge can improve your striking power and overall skill. Applying the principles of kinematics and dynamics to your regular practice will eventually allow you to execute more effective striking techniques.

THE HAMMERHAND STRIKE
Wing Chun Kung Fu's Most Underrated Fighting Technique

by Todd Tei • Photos by Todd Tei • May 1995

The hammerhand strike is perhaps the most underrated technique in the *wing chun* kung fu system. But although the technique is not as popular as a straight punch, finger jab or kick, it is just as effective as those maneuvers. The hammerhand strike is a welcome addition to any fighter's arsenal because it is used immediately after a block or deflection, while your hands are poised to strike.

The strike is called the hammerhand because you hit the opponent with the bottom portion of your closed hand, without using the knuckles. Have you ever hit down on a table with your fist when you were frustrated? The hammerhand strike is executed in a similar manner, except you use it to strike your opponent's ribs, temple, jaw, stomach or neck. The hammerhand strike is best used as a follow-up to a parrying technique. For example, after executing an inside or outside slap-hand block (*pak sao*), the hammerhand is an effective counterattack because the underside of your hand is already positioned to strike your opponent's face. After parry-

In this sequence, the defender (left) parries (1) an attacker's punch and counters with a hammerhand to the midsection. He follows (2) with a simultaneous hammerhand to the back and kick to the knee.

ing, you simply make a fist as your hand moves to smash your adversary's face. The parry hammerhand combination is actually more effective than a parry/backfist combination, which requires two separate movements, slowing your response time.

The wing chun hammerhand strike can be utilized in other effective ways. The technique can be delivered upward, with your palm to the sky

The hammerhand strike can be delivered in a variety of ways. In this sequence, the defender (left) parries (1) an opponent's punch with a slap block and converts (2) the parry into a hammerhand, using the bottom of the fist as the striking surface. The defender follows (3) with a simultaneous punch to the face and kick to the groin.

in a fist, or it can be executed with the knuckles facing down, or in any direction in which sufficient contact is maintained with the target. The hammerhand strike can also be substituted for a knifehand. For example, after parrying an opponent's punch, you could deliver a hammerhand strike to the side of his neck or jaw.

Hammerhand Grabbing Techniques

After executing a hammerhand strike, the wing chun practitioner can easily transition into a grabbing maneuver with the same hand. For example, if an opponent attacks with a punch, you can counter with a hammerhand to the temple. After striking, open your hand and pull the opponent's head forward into a knee smash or straight kick. Or you could follow with a hammerhand to the opponent's ribs, allowing you to bring your arm up quickly into a palm block (*tan sao*) before striking your opponent again.

Or these techniques can be varied and used together as effective combinations. For instance, you could transition from the tan sao palm block into a hammerhand strike, then switch to a grabbing maneuver. Another variation would be to substitute a hammerhand for the palm strike, or deliver the palm strike first and then convert your open hand into a closed hammerhand strike.

Hammerhand Slams

If you are engaged in close-range combat and do not wish to paralyze your opponent with a punch, try pushing him away with a "hammerhand slam." The forearm, instead of the fist, can be used in tight quarters to strike the opponent's neck, chest or jaw. Similar movements can be found in *tai chi chuan* and can be followed by a palm strike to the opponent's face or can be used in conjunction with the hammerhand slam.

Hammerhand Training

The hammerhand can be practiced against a canvas bag, wooden dummy, or anything solid that can absorb blows without being damaged or causing injury. Practice the technique with your knuckles facing both downward and upward. And don't forget to use proper wing chun striking technique, snapping your arms as if they were a whip, hitting the target and bouncing back.

Choy Li Fut Hammerhand Strike

Wing chun is not the only kung fu system that utilizes a hammerhand strike. The technique is also found in *choy li fut*, as well as several other styles. In choy li fut, the hammerhand is known as *pek chui*, or "hammerfist strike." Choy li fut's hammerhand strike relies on the coordination of the practitioner's waist, stance and footwork to generate power for the blow. Choy li fut's stances are broad and low, as compared to wing chun stances, which are not as economical and compact.

Wing chun has four basic stances: horse stance, side stance, *biuma* or dart stance and large horse stance. Most of the style's stances are high and less rigid than those in other martial arts. For example, if a wing chun stylist is defending against an opponent's straight punch, he would likely parry the blow with a pak sao slap hand and follow through with a hammerhand strike with the same arm. A choy li fut stylist, on the other hand, would use evasive footwork and circular spinning blocks to avoid the opponent's punching attack and would then follow with a hammerfist strike.

The two kung fu styles also feature different arm positions for the hammerhand strike. In choy li fut, the practitioner extends his entire arm when delivering the hammerhand. Wing chun stylists, however, prefer shorter arm extensions, enabling them to employ techniques quickly and efficiently.

Developing Chi

Proper channeling of *chi* (internal energy) can add power to your hammerhand strike. Chi can be developed through a series of progressive meditation, breathing and *chi kung* (breathing exercises) drills. You can begin by standing in a horse stance with your hands at waist level. Move your hands into palm-strike position in front of you. Exhale and then bring your hands back to your waist. Now inhale.

You will feel a building tension and power inside you, like water moving through a hose. It's the feeling of chi connecting to your spirit and flowing through your body.

Chi kung exercises purportedly originated at China's legendary Shaolin Temple and were handed down from family to family. Those who learned the information took an oath to guard the then-secret exercises. Chi kung can be used not only to increase the chi power in a practitioner's techniques but also to heal.

More often, however, chi kung is associated with the remarkable ability to strike an opponent only inches away with devastating power. Instead of pulling the arm back to generate enough distance to execute a punch, chi kung practitioners have learned to concentrate their energy in a small space and produce as much or more power in a blow. A perfect example of this phenomenon is Bruce Lee's famous "one-inch punch," which could send an opponent reeling backward despite the close beginning point of the technique. The hammerhand strike can be a valuable addition to any wing chun stylist's fighting arsenal. It is most effectively applied as a follow-up maneuver to a parry, but it can also be utilized in conjunction with a grabbing technique or in combination with a variety of other maneuvers. Learning to channel your chi can add power to your hammerhand strike, producing potentially lethal results.

The hammerhand strike can be used in conjunction with a grabbing technique, as illustrated in this sequence. The defender (left) parries (1) a punch and converts (2) the parry to a hammerhand strike to the opponent's temple. The defender follows (3) by converting the hammerhand to a grab and forcing the opponent's head into a kick.

THE INFAMOUS "KARATE CHOP"
The Public's Fascination With the Knifehand Strike Overshadows Its Effectiveness

by Chuck Taylor • Photos by Chuck Taylor • July 1995

The karate "chop." It's the most famous technique in the martial arts. How many times have you heard somebody joke, "Get back, or I'll karate chop you." Barney Fife was always slicing the Mayberry air with his chops, warning suspects that his hands were registered as weapons. Everyone knows how to karate chop, from the highest black belt to the lowest nerd. You just shape your hand into a blade, tuck your thumb, and voilà! You have a karate chop ready to carve up the nearest opponent.

If you train in a self-defense system that includes the chop, or knifehand, as it is commonly called, you know there is a lot more to this technique than the average person realizes. It takes years of conditioning to execute safely and years of practice to deliver effectively.

Exactly when the karate chop was introduced to North America has long been debated. Some individuals claim the knifehand arrived with Chinese immigrants brought to the United States in the 1800s to work on railroad projects. Others insist that Japanese immigrants brought *jujutsu* to America's shores before the Chinese "coolies" arrived, and therefore likely taught the *shuto* technique to Westerners. And some believe the technique arrived with U.S. servicemen returning from Asia after World War II with newfound martial arts skills, taught to them by Okinawan and Japanese masters.

It is a fact that judo and jujutsu gained widespread publicity in the United States after World War II. To the uninformed American public,

The knifehand can be employed palm-up to strike (1-2) an opponent on the side of the head.

One way to toughen your hand to deliver powerful knifehand strikes is to practice against a *makiwara*.

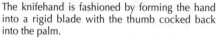

The knifehand is fashioned by forming the hand into a rigid blade with the thumb cocked back into the palm.

judo and karate became synonymous with a single technique—the judo or karate chop. The technique began to pop up all over the country. Professional wrestlers used it in their matches. Mr. Moto used it in his movies. And the general populace brandished it in homes and offices across the United States.

The late *kyokushin* karate master Masutatsu Oyama also had a hand in America's fascination with the knifehand technique. In the 1950s, Oyama toured the United States as part of a professional wrestling team called the "Togo Brothers." Oyama impressed the public with his amazing skill at breaking boards, bricks and rocks with the edge of his bare hand, and he even demonstrated his abilities before a packed house at Madison Square

Or it can delivered from the side, palm-down, to strike (3-4) the neck.

The knifehand can be thrust directly ahead to strike (1-2) an opponent in the collarbone.

Garden in New York City. Oyama was well-known in Japan for fighting bulls with his bare hands, and he reportedly used knifehand strikes to break the horns off of some of the animals.

Most karate systems make use of several different striking points on the hand, from knuckles to fingertips to the inner edge of the hand. But the knifehand technique, which utilizes the outside edge of the hand as the striking surface, continues to be the technique the public most closely associates with the martial arts. Let's take a closer look at the combat applicability of this technique that has so captured the public's imagination.

The knifehand strike is a strong, versatile technique that is found in virtually all Asian fighting systems, regardless of their country of origin. The technique has been refined over a period of hundreds of years and is second only to the fist among popular hand strikes.

When Americans were first introduced to the knifehand strike, the general assumption was that the hand was merely held flat, with the thumb sticking out, and that the technique was employed like a club, moving

The knifehand can be utilized as a blocking technique, such as this vertical knifehand block (1-2), which deflects an attacker's punch.

downward from overhead to hammer the opponent into submission. As you might guess, it is not nearly as simple as that. The hand is not just held flat; it is formed into a weapon.

In Oyama's kyokushin system, this is accomplished by cocking the thumb back as if it were trying to retract into the hand. At the same time, the little finger extends while the index, middle and ring fingers try to withdraw into the palm, just as the thumb did. The concept of the fingers extending or withdrawing is actually used to obtain proper tension in the hand. When performed correctly, the edge of the hand and the palm become very firm or dense. This edge can be forged into a weapon by repeatedly striking a heavy bag or *makiwara* (padded punching post). Thusly conditioned, the knifehand becomes a versatile and effective weapon in a martial artist's combat arsenal. It can be delivered in a thrusting or slashing manner, or it can serve as a blocking technique, thwarting and redirecting an opponent's attack.

The knifehand can be delivered in a variety of ways to a number of targets. Palm-down or palm-up knifehand strikes can be easily targeted to an opponent's ribs, temple or neck. If you are being attacked from the rear, you can unleash an upward-moving knifehand strike back into your opponent's testicles. You can strike an opponent's collarbone by driving the knifehand directly forward, or you can deliver the technique in a downward, chopping manner to the collarbone or other targets.

As mentioned earlier, the knifehand is highly effective as a blocking tool. The most common knifehand block is *shuto uke*, which is initiated by bringing the blocking hand across your body so that the palm is cupping your ear. From there, the hand and arm swing outward, and the knifehand deflects the opponent's oncoming appendage.

There are several subtle variations of this block. A vertical knifehand block, known as *tate shuto uke*, can be executed by performing the same arm motion, but with the blocking hand held in a vertical position. When a subtle hooking or pulling motion is added to the original knifehand block, it becomes a *kake shuto uke* technique.

*   *   *

Although the so-called "chop" is not the central technique of karate, as many people mistakenly believe, it is nonetheless an integral component of many self-defense systems and can be implemented to either strike an opponent or ward off his attacks.

10 HAND STRIKES OF WING CHUN KUNG FU
Turn Your Fingers, Hands, Forearms and Elbows Into Deadly Weapons

by Todd Shawn Tei • Photos by Todd Shawn Tei • December 1995

The Shaolin Temple in China's Hunan province is considered by martial arts historians to be the site where many kung fu styles originated. According to legend, it was a Buddhist monk named Bodhidharma who suggested that the temple's clerics train in kung fu so they would be able to defend the monastery against those who wanted to pillage and destroy it. Bodhidharma, who was of Indian descent, taught his disciples a form of yoga that was somehow converted to a martial art. The combat system featured fighting tactics that originated from observing natural defensive methods of a variety of animals, including tigers, dragons, cranes, snakes and leopards.

One of the kung fu systems taught at the Shaolin Temple was *wing chun*, which was developed by a nun named Ng Mui, who named the style after her first student, Yim Wing Chun. Rather than create an entirely new style, Ng merely combined the most effective and economical elements from all of the temple's fighting arts into one system of self-defense called wing chun, which meant "beautiful springtime."

Instead of relying on brute strength or forceful blocks, wing chun practitioners attempt to redirect their opponents' energy and/or power and use it against them. The hand movements are relaxed and never stiff or rigid.

The following are 10 of wing chun's most potent hand strikes:

• **Palm strike**—This is probably the most frequently used hand technique in wing chun. It can be executed immediately after a *pak sao* (slap-hand block) technique or a *lop sao* (grabbing hand) maneuver. There are many variations of the palm strike. It can be executed with your palm in a horizontal or vertical position, or with the palm facing up or toward the ground. The palm strike can also be delivered in a side (knifehand) position to an opponent's jaw or neck.

• **Side palm strike**—This technique is usually employed after the wing chun stylist has performed a *tan sao* (palm-up block) maneuver. The wing chun practitioner can deflect an opponent's punch with a tan sao technique and simultaneously counterattack with a side palm strike to the jaw or temple.

• **Knifehand strike**—This rapid, knifelike chopping hand technique is often used to strike the opponent's neck, ribs or face. The technique is

Wing chun's hand strikes include the backfist (1), knifehand (2), spearhand (3), straight punch (4), hammerhand (5) and elbow smash (6).

most commonly employed after a pak sao slap hand has redirected an opponent's strike.

• **Wrist strike**—One of wing chun's most classical weapons, this blow is generally used as the first strike in a rapid combination of hand techniques. The wrist strike is often delivered to the opponent's chest, leaving him vulnerable to a follow-up palm strike and a wing chun straight punch. Each of these techniques is delivered at close range with the same hand.

• **Hammerhand strike**—Before there was the backfist, there was the hammerhand strike. This hand technique is a favorite among traditional wing chun stylists, but most people who study the system today don't realize how useful the hammerhand can be in their self-defense arsenal.

In this self-defense sequence, the *wing chun* practitioner (right) employs (1) a slap block to deflect his attacker's punch while simultaneously counterattacking with a straight punch to the face. The wing chun stylist slides his right arm down to redirect (2) his opponent's punching arm and delivers a left straight punch to the cheekbone. The defender switches arms again, connecting (3) with a right straight punch to the face and then finishes (4) with a left knifehand strike to the throat.

Have you ever hit your hand down on a table when you were frustrated or angry? If so, you likely remember the power that generated from the bottom portion of your hand. To perform the hammerhand strike, make a fist, with your knuckles facing up or toward the ground. Then, swing the fist downward, forward or backward, using the bottom part of your hand as the striking surface. The hammerhand strike is particularly effective as a follow-up technique to a palm-up deflection block (tan sao).

• **Backfist**—This technique is not used in traditional wing chun circles too often yet is a highly effective and explosive hand strike. The backfist is generally targeted to the opponent's ribs, temple, jaw or face. It is particularly useful after you grab your opponent's arm with a lop sao technique. The blow is more effective if you slant the backfist at an angle instead of delivering a straight or horizontal technique.

• **Forearm strike**—If executed properly, this strike is like being hit with a baseball bat. As your opponent advances, you simply parry his striking arm and execute a forearm strike to his chest, ribs, throat or groin. Keep your hand in a knifehand configuration, and strike with the portion of your arm from the wrist to the elbow.

• **Spearhand strike**—By placing your fingers closely together to form a point, you can effectively strike the opponent's eyes, throat, solar plexus or floating ribs with this technique. The spearhand strike is quite lethal and could blind or severely injure an opponent. It should therefore be used only in potentially life-threatening circumstances.

Wing Chun's elbow strike can be delivered horizontally (1) or vertically (2) with equal effectiveness.

Two other *wing chun* hand techniques are the palm strike, which can be delivered in pairs (1), and the forearm strike (2), which can be directed to the opponent's neck or chest.

• **Elbow strike**—This is a powerful and potentially devastating technique. You can deliver the elbow strike in either a horizontal or vertical manner. By twisting your hips as you move into the technique, you can intensify the strike. Targets include the opponent's jaw, temple, cheek or chin.

• **Straight punch**—Wing chun is noted for its straight punch. The technique is delivered by keeping your hand completely open and relaxed until the moment of impact, when your hand quickly snaps upward into a jolting straight punch. The punch always travels in a straight line to its target, making it an extremely quick and effective technique. Conversely, the hook punch, which is so popular in boxing, is never used in wing chun because it is too slow and the opponent can see it coming.

* * *

Palms, elbows, knifehands, spearhands and punches—wing chun makes good use of the body's armaments, turning virtually any appendage into a potentially deadly weapon. By learning wing chun kung fu, you, too, can possess a lethal arsenal of hand strikes, thus preparing yourself for virtually any combat situation.

VITAL-POINT ATTACKS
Strikes to the Eyes, Groin and Throat Are a Woman's Equalizer in a Fight

by John Bishop • Photos by John Bishop • June 1996

Even in today's modern times, some karate instructors still believe that women have little or no place in the martial arts. They think women are too small, too weak or too feminine to keep up with the men in class. Some individuals believe women should stick to softer arts, like *tai chi chuan*, or train at schools that specialize in women-only classes.

However, training only with women can cause more harm than good for the average female student. If a woman is attacked, the chances are good that her assailant will be male. For this reason, women need to train with men to get a realistic idea of what it takes to defeat an assailant on the street.

Obviously, most women cannot expect to match brute strength with a male attacker. A woman, therefore, needs to be smarter than her male opponent and target her techniques to what are known as "vital points," which can help even the odds. If an average-size woman punches a well-muscled or large man anywhere other than a vital area, he will most likely shrug off the blow and resume his attack. By targeting vital points, however, the woman can cause debilitating injuries to a much larger and stronger opponent.

Where Are the Vital Points?

Vital points are areas on the human body that can be easily damaged by a minimum amount of force. For self-defense purposes, these points would include the eyes, groin, throat, solar plexus, knee, shin and temple.

Groin Strikes

Whether you are a 120-pound weakling or a 300-pound professional football player, if you take a shot to the groin, you're going to go down or, at the very least, double over in pain and remain incapacitated for a time. And it doesn't matter whether an adult male or a 10-year-old girl delivered the groin strike.

Most men make a point of protecting their groin during a fight with another man, but they may be more lackadaisical about defending themselves when their opponent is a woman. Many times, a rapist expects no resistance from his female victim. In fact, much of his gratification may come from terrorizing the woman and imposing his physical dominance

In this *kajukenbo* defense, an assailant reaches for a woman, who quickly knocks (1) his hands to the outside and then counterattacks with a poke (2) to the eyes.

over her. This tendency toward overconfidence makes him less suspicious of—and less prepared for—a groin strike from his would-be victim.

Because the groin is protected on either side by the legs, strikes to the male reproductive organs have to be delivered either straight in or straight up between the legs. If the victim is standing, a front snap kick may be the quickest, most effective way to strike her attacker's groin. If she has been forced to her knees, she can execute a punch or grab to the opponent's gonads. If the assailant is straddling her on the ground, he is sure to expose his genitalia at some point. When he does, he is quite vulnerable to a kick or a grab.

Any properly placed blow to the groin can cause pain, shock, loss of breath, nausea, vomiting, unconsciousness and, possibly, even death.

Throat Strikes

The throat is another area that can be easily damaged with minimal force. The two most important life-sustaining elements—blood and oxygen—flow through the throat. Without either of these components, the body will die within minutes. The air passage, veins and nerves in the throat are highly sensitive; a strike or grab to the region can cause great pain and temporarily disable an attacker.

She follows with a palm heel (3) to the jaw and a front snap kick (4) to the groin. She can now effect an escape (5) from her incapacitated attacker.

In this *kajukenbo* defense against an attacker's lapel grab (1), the female defender responds by clawing (2) her assailant's eyes as he pulls her toward him. She then grabs his hair and pulls him into a knee smash (3) to the groin.

The front portion of the throat is the best area to target. The frontal region can be struck with a knifehand or a fore-knuckle punch, or the victim can grab the throat in a ripping motion. Most men do not worry about protecting their throat during a fight. A victim facing her attacker, on the side of her attacker or on the ground with an assailant bending over her can strike the throat.

Eye Strikes

The eyes are perhaps the best targets a woman can attack when defending herself. The eyes can be easily poked, clawed or raked with keys or other hand-held items. If you can touch someone's face, you are close enough to effectively attack the eyes.

There is no stronger sense of helplessness than to suddenly lose your sight. Along with the excruciating pain of an eye attack comes temporary or permanent blindness. This twofold debilitation should be enough to allow a victim to break free and escape while her attacker is incapacitated.

* * *

Although there are other vital points—such as the knees, shins, temples and solar plexus—the groin, throat and eyes remain the most potentially debilitating areas for such strikes. On the surface, these techniques may seem too brutal and/or cruel to use, yet they are necessary evils in the arsenal of any woman who hopes to defend herself in an attack. Any man who would attack a woman is extremely dangerous and deserves whatever he gets. If that happens to be a strike to his groin, throat or eyes, so be it.

THE TRUTH ABOUT KARATE'S ONE-STRIKE KILL

by Dave Lowry • September 1996

Ikken hisatsu is an oft-heard expression in the karate *dojo* (school). It is usually translated as "one-strike kill" or "the ability to kill with a single strike." After karate was introduced to the United States, a great many wild tales were attached to this phrase. Among them was the notion that karate was so devastating as a fighting art that an experienced practitioner was capable of dealing—with a single punch or a well-placed "karate chop"—a blow that would cause an opponent's instant death. This was one reason given for not conducting full-contact training in karate; it was considered too dangerous. If just one punch could permanently put out the lights of the recipient, you obviously could not have karate practitioners attacking one another in an uncontrolled fashion in class.

Of course, many martial artists wondered whether the strikes they were learning really were that deadly. They couldn't ask their teacher; such a question might seem disrespectful to their art. Having witnessed or performed feats of breaking, many students may have reasoned that, if a punch can go through a stack of boards or bricks, why couldn't that same punch destroy a human being?

It wasn't too many years before some doubts about the "one-strike kill" began to surface. More than one karate practitioner must have thought, "I have made heavy contact with an opponent in tournaments and in practice, and while I may have broken his nose, blackened his eye or even knocked him unconscious, he's still alive today. How can that be?"

In the 1970s, some martial artists began experimenting with what was called "full-contact karate." Although the fighters were heavily padded, the supposedly deadly strikes of karate didn't seem to be living up to their reputation in the ring. The famous "one-strike kill" rapidly found itself shelved right next to the stories about the tooth fairy. Today, thanks in part to the plethora of mixed-martial arts fighting events, no one takes seriously the notion that a single punch or kick from a karate exponent can actually take a life.

And that's a step forward in our understanding of karate in the West. Because ikken hisatsu was never understood in Japan to mean what Western-ers have come to think it means. Ikken hisatsu does not mean that a single blow will cause death. It means that one must, in a real fight, adopt the *attitude* that a single blow can cause death. The difference is enormous.

Think back to the scraps that occasionally unfolded on the schoolyard as a youth. A few punches might be thrown, and then the bouts generally became a matter of close-quarter grappling. The combatants may have been very angry with each other and waded into battle with deep sincerity to injure one another, but no one expected the fight to end in death. The same can be said of most bar fights.

The philosophy of karate takes an entirely different view toward fighting. As an Okinawan karate teacher once said, "If it isn't worth dying for, it isn't worth fighting for." The mentality of karate encourages three approaches to conflict. The first is that you avoid the circumstances that are likely to end in a fight. This harkens back to the old idea about crossing the street rather than walking right into the middle of a bunch of potential thugs, or looking into the back seat of your car before entering to make sure no one's hiding there.

The second approach to conflict calls for using your wits to de-escalate an imminent fight before it starts. This approach could entail talking quietly in the face of a threat or shouting boldly to destroy the potential attacker's

---

Today, thanks in part to the plethora of mixed-martial arts events, no one takes seriously the notion that a single punch or kick from a karate exponent can actually take a life.

---

initiative and nerve before he makes the first move. These tactics may psychologically disarm the conflict.

The third approach—ikken hisatsu—is used only after the other two have failed.

Adopting the attitude of ikken hisatsu means to be irretrievably committed to destroying the opponent (or possibly being destroyed yourself). It means accepting coldly and with knowledge aforethought the fact that someone will die in the next few moments. It means that you are willing to attack with total commitment.

Yet ikken hisatsu is not a testosterone-fueled *kamikaze* charge. It is not a matter of bravado or phony patriotism or *machismo*. It's a calculated, logical and premeditated attack. The martial artist is committing himself to possible destruction, with the expectation that his enemy is going to do the same.

Ikken hisatsu is a concept that exists on a different plane entirely from ordinary living. It is in the realm where life and death come together. The martial artist who has come face to face with the true meaning of "one-strike death" does not carry with him the foolish thought that he has the mystical power to take a life with but a single blow. He may, if he is lucky or if his opponent is a very poor fighter, be able to accomplish that. He may also, if he should happen to encounter an enemy vastly more talented than himself, be killed just as quickly.

These are, as more than one great Japanese swordsman has written, matters of fate and must be accepted. What distinguishes the martial artist who has penetrated the depths of meaning behind ikken hisatsu is this: He is willing, if all else fails, to enter into a conflict with his entire being, without reservation. With one strike—or with a dozen—he may kill or be killed. But whatever it takes, that's what he is going to do. That is ikken hisatsu.

ELBOW STRIKES OF TANG SOO DO
The Most Lethal Close-Range Counterattack in the Martial Arts?

by Thomas M. Cox • Photos by Thomas M. Cox • December 1996

Jumping, whirling, spinning kicks to the head—this is the image that generally comes to mind when someone mentions the fighting systems of Korean heritage. And rightfully so. Most of the Korean martial arts are noted for their impressive array of kicking techniques.

Kicks, however, are generally only effective when delivered from long range, and there are three other distances—punching, trapping and grappling range—to consider when fighting. Obviously, hand strikes are the techniques of choice at punching range, but what is the preferred blow at trapping and grappling distance? In the Korean art *tang soo do*, the answer is: an elbow strike.

Once a fighter has penetrated his opponent's outer perimeter, weapons other than kicks are required. At the innermost ring of defense, tang soo do stylists use the elbow as the basic striking weapon. In close quarters, when you can virtually smell your adversary's breath, it is often impossible to fully extend a fist and position yourself for an effective punch. Elbows are much closer to the center of the body than the hands and can therefore be utilized with greater power and speed in a confined area.

There are two basic striking points on the elbow when it is employed as an offensive weapon. One striking surface is that portion of the forearm nearest the elbow joint. This area is generally utilized in one of two ways:

If an opponent grabs (1) his lapel, the *tang soo do* stylist (right) can counterattack (2) by twisting his body, raising his right arm and striking the assailant's wrists with a downward elbow smash. A follow-up elbow strike (3) to the chin should incapacitate the attacker.

133

It can be swung on an outside-to-inside arc (right to left when using the right elbow), or in an upward arc. The outside-to-inside arc is usually implemented in an entirely horizontal motion, while the upward arc is generally employed in a strictly vertical manner. In both circumstances, the hip on the same side as the elbow (the right hip if striking with the right elbow) is thrust forward to provide the power behind the strike.

Two opponents face off (1) in this self-defense sequence, and the *tang soo do* stylist (right) sidesteps and blocks (2) the attacker's roundhouse kick. The defender grabs and pins (3) the kicker's leg while delivering (4) a powerful downward elbow smash to the back of the knee.

That portion of the upper arm that is nearest the elbow joint serves as the second striking surface in basic elbow attacks. This area is generally employed when the elbow is swung on an inside-to-outside arc (left to right when using the right elbow), or in a downward arc. The power for this type of strike is provided by pulling the hip on that side through the target. The inside-to-outside arc is generally made on a strictly horizontal plane, while the downward strike is delivered on a vertical plane.

Although the tang soo do practitioner can spin as he initiates one of the horizontal arc strikes—adding momentum to the blows—elbow attacks can also be directed in a backward motion without spinning.

Either elbow can be delivered with considerable force by holding the arm straight out in front, palm up, then pulling the elbow back, closely passing the striker's body. This type of attack is especially suited to a two-handed strike, or what is referred to as a "reinforced" elbow attack. Unlike punches and kicks, an elbow attack can be supported with the tang soo do stylist's nonstriking hand. The practitioner simply places his open nonstriking hand over the fist of the arm that is being used for the elbow attack.

Elbows are much closer to the center of the body than the hands and can therefore be utilized with greater power and speed in a confined area.

There are two benefits to reinforcing an elbow strike. First, the extra support lends additional power to the blow by pushing the elbow toward the target with the opposite hand. Second, by placing both hands in such close proximity (that is, the open hand over the clenched fist), the entire body works as a single unit. The hips move in unison with the elbow; thus, the lower body is working in harmony with the upper body. Added mass and greater acceleration are therefore the result, bringing greater power to bear on the target.

Tang soo do practitioners utilize a principle called the "three C's"—contact, capture and control—when dealing with self-defense technique applications. "Contact" refers to blocking or thwarting the opponent's attack. This is quite often described simply as "avoiding" the attack, because the basic premise of self-defense is not to be struck by the opponent. Contact is necessary, however, to establish the attacker's position relative to the defender. The contact is usually in the form of a block, although it may merely be a touch between the two opponents as the defender sidesteps his assailant.

In this scenario, an attacker (left) has grabbed (1) the *tang soo do* stylist by the wrist. The defender reacts by stepping forward (2) and lowering his center of gravity, which in turn negates the effectiveness of the hold.

"Capture" introduces the element of attachment to an attacker, which is a natural continuation of the altercation after contact is made with an opponent. The attachment, or capture mode, is the first step toward controlling the attacker.

Although the tang soo do practitioner can spin as he initiates one of the horizontal arc strikes — adding momentum to the blows — elbow attacks can also be directed in a backward motion without spinning.

"Control" means just that—controlling your opponent so he cannot harm you. This final phase of the conflict results in placing the assailant into a predicament that leaves the defender in charge of what happens

Continuing forward, the tang soo do stylist escapes the hold by twisting his body as he delivers (3) an elbow smash to the opponent's temple. The defender continues pivoting, striking (4) his attacker under the chin with a spinning elbow smash.

next. This could be a joint lock or other submission hold that leads to a finishing strike or perhaps a choke hold.

* * *

Much like the golf adage "Drive for show, and putt for dough," it is clear that even the most spectacular kicker needs to possess solid close-range fighting skills, as well. Fancy flying kicks of Korean heritage are great, but they will be of little use to the defender if the fight moves—as it usually does—to trapping or grappling range. In close-quarters, there is no more effective or potentially lethal counterattack than a tang soo do elbow strike.

DO YOU KNOW HOW TO PUNCH PROPERLY?
Six Tips for Better Striking Skills
by Tom Callos • Photos by Tobiah Hoogs • March 1997

If you have taken more than a week's worth of martial arts lessons, you have no doubt learned a punching technique or two. Perhaps you have practiced thousands, or even millions, of punches since you started training in the martial arts. But do you know how to punch *effectively*?

The way you punch, and the way you train to be a better puncher, depend greatly on *why* you're punching in the first place.

There are basically three different reasons people learn how to punch: for fun and/or conditioning, for sport and for self-defense.

• **Punching for fun and/or conditioning**—If you are practicing punching simply because you enjoy it or because you want to get into better condition, you are developing skills similar to those used by professional fighters, but without having to suffer the pain that comes from mixing it up in the ring with an opponent. If you are training for these reasons, you

---

You will rarely be able to incapacitate an opponent with a single blow, no matter how strong or skilled you are.

---

probably aren't interested in sparring much. You may simply like the way it feels to hit a hanging bag or focus mitt. Such training will help you become a much better puncher—and you won't lose all your teeth. Plus, you will improve your fitness as well as your ability to defend yourself.

• **Punching for sport**—Punching for competition is completely different than punching for fun or conditioning. The punching tools you need to develop are dictated by the rules of the martial sport in which you are competing. If you are fighting in open martial arts tournaments, you are primarily interested in developing punches that possess little or no power because of the rules regarding excessive contact. Conversely, if you are competing as a kickboxer, you want as much power in your punches as possible so you will have the capability of knocking out your opponent. Improved physical fitness and self-defense skills are byproducts of sport punching practice.

• **Punching for self-defense**—Your goal is to avoid getting hurt when punching for reasons of self-defense. There is no ring and no referee, and there are no rules to consider. You're free to hit your adversary with any part of your fist, fingers, open hand, forearm or elbow. And you can strike your opponent with as much power as you desire. Punches can be used to set up a kick, a takedown, a choke or a mad dash to freedom.

The following six tips will help you become a more effective puncher, regardless of whether you are training for fun, fitness, sport or self-defense:

• **Wrap your hands**—It is advisable to protect your knuckle with boxing hand wraps and gloves whenever you punch on a heavy bag or focus pad. To become an expert puncher, you are going to have to perform thousands of repetitions on bags and/or other training equipment, so it is essential—and smart—to protect your skin and bones against unnecessary injuries.

• **Learn the basics**—Add the basic boxing techniques—cross, hook and uppercut—to your repertoire, and then perfect them through constant practice. This does not mean you have to abandon the traditional karate strikes—reverse punch, backfist, ridgehand, etc.—you may have

Focus-mitt drills with a partner are a great way to improve punching skills, whether working on right crosses (1), left hooks (2) or uppercuts (3).

The 90-Day Punching Program

Javier Mendez, the former International Sport Karate Association light-cruiserweight and light-heavyweight champion of the world designed the following training program. Mendez, who owns a professional kickboxing record of 22-2 with 14 knockouts, believes his 90-day program can help any martial artist develop more punching fluidity, snap and speed.

Beginners program (for martial artists with less than two years of training):
• Mondays and Wednesdays—three to four three-minute rounds of shadowboxing in front of a mirror. The goal is to improve your punching form and fluidity.
• Tuesdays and Thursdays—three to four rounds of heavy-bag or focus-mitt punching. Concentrate on your form, speed and power. The entire workout, with short rests between each round, should take 15 minutes.

Intermediate and advanced program:
• Three to four rounds of shadowboxing to hone your technique.
• Three to four rounds on the heavy bag to develop power.
• Two rounds on a double-ended speed ball to develop power.
• Two to three rounds on a speed bag and three to four rounds on the focus mitts, both of which develop timing, accuracy and conditioning.
Perform the drills two to five days a week. The entire workout, with rests between rounds, should take 30 to 45 minutes.

already learned; you should be versatile enough to include both methods in your arsenal.

• **Body movement and combinations**—The difference between getting hit or being missed by an opponent's blow can be a matter of micro-inches. Knowing how to move your body out of the way of an attack is a skill boxers learn to perfect, but martial artists often ignore. Boxers are taught to bob and weave to avoid an opponent's punches, and the very nature of their body movement allows them to set up powerful counterpunches.

Former world kickboxing champion Javier Mendez says, "Karate fighters are usually too stiff in their punching style and body movement. My advice is to loosen up and learn how to use the body during attacks and defense. Fighters who know how to move can be frustratingly hard to hit—even for the best punchers."

You will rarely be able to incapacitate an opponent with a single blow, no matter how strong or skilled you are. Therefore, knowing how to set up combinations of techniques is essential. The combined effect of body movement and a flurry of well-placed punches are what make boxers formidable.

• **Train with focus mitts**—Focus mitts or pads are an essential part of learning how to deliver effective punching combinations. Focus mitts are held by a partner, who can maneuver them about in any way he sees fit, thus allowing you to strike a moving target. It is much more realistic training than hitting a stationary heavy bag. Focus-mitt training also enables you to get accustomed to facing an opponent at a realistic fighting distance.

The way you punch, and the way you train to be a better puncher, depend greatly on why you're punching in the first place.

Troy Dorsey, who is the only man to ever hold world titles in both boxing and kickboxing, claims, "[Focus-mitt training] is second only to sparring in my workouts."

• **Shadowbox**—Former North American kickboxing champion Dan Magnus claims shadowboxing was a big key to his success as a fighter. "Shadowboxing teaches you how to miss punches and keep flowing," Magnus says. "If you punch a bag 100 times, you hit it 100 times. But in an actual bout, you miss many of your punches. I've seen guys who could hit the heavy bag like a sledgehammer, but when they miss with a punch, they fall on their face."

• **Take boxing lessons**—As difficult as this may be to swallow, you will probably learn more about punching after a month of boxing lessons than you would after a year of traditional *taekwondo* or karate training. Boxing doesn't possess the variety of techniques the martial arts do, but by studying the so-called "sweet science," you will be able to hit harder, faster and more effectively.

THE INFIGHTING ARSENAL OF GOJU-RYU KARATE
by Scott Lenzi • Photos by Scott Lenzi • June 1997

Although *goju-ryu* includes many "soft" blocking techniques and movements in its fighting arsenal, it is, like most karate styles that originated on Okinawa, best known for its powerful striking arsenal. And perhaps the most potent blows in goju-ryu's repertoire of techniques are its elbow and knee strikes.

Goju-ryu, and particularly the *shorei-kan* style of goju-ryu, is a system of karate geared for close-range fighting, and it therefore depends heavily on the use of the knees and the elbows. This article will explain how goju-ryu practitioners utilize elbows and knees as both weapons and blocking tools.

Goju-Ryu Elbow Strikes and Blocks

Elbows are both versatile and highly effective when utilized as striking or blocking implements at close range, and a variety of elbow strikes and blocks can be found in all of the classical *kata* (solo training patterns) of goju-ryu.

Elbow strikes fall into two basic categories: those that move perpendicular to the body's vertical center axis (head to toe), and those that are in line with the vertical center axis.

Goju-ryu creator Chojun Miyagi's *gekisai dai ichi* kata contains one of the more common uses of the elbow in karate. This rising striking technique, called *tate enpi*, follows the body's center axis and is often employed as a follow-up to a front kick (*mae geri*). Seikichi Toguchi, a senior student of Miyagi and founder of the shorei-kan school of goju-ryu, created a two-man training form for this kata to allow practical and safe practice of the form's techniques, including tate enpi.

Goju-ryu's *seiunchin* kata contains a block that utilizes the practitioner's elbow to defend against a tate enpi strike. This block rises in the same manner as a tate enpi blow and forces the opponent's elbow to continue in its same line, thus causing the attacker to lose his balance while creating an opening for a counterattack.

Yet another defensive elbow technique occurs in the seiunchin kata for the same tate enpi strike when the defender pivots and simultaneously executes a lateral block/strike combination to counter the attacker's rising elbow.

Another variety of elbow strikes can be found in a number of classical karate kata, including *saifa* and *seisan*. These techniques move perpendicularly to the goju-ryu stylist's central axis. The only difference between the perpendicular elbow strikes in saifa and seisan is their completion point, which is critical, when analyzing how each elbow strike is best used.

The seisan elbow attack—which targets the opponent's rib cage and the area just below it on the sides of his body—emphasizes striking with the forearm instead of the elbow point, which is utilized in the saifa version. Both of these perpendicular techniques are usually executed from a *shikodachi* (horse stance) posture because the targets are generally located in the middle of the opponent's body.

Defensive elbow techniques for these perpendicular elbow attacks are derived from goju-ryu kata such as seiunchin, *kururunfa* and *shisochin*. From kururunfa, a perpendicular elbow strike like that seen in seisan is defended by executing a *kuri uke* elbow block in a downward manner, which sets the attacker up for a lateral elbow counterstrike.

Goju-Ryu Knee Strikes and Blocks

The *hiza geri* knee kick, and its many variations, is the goju-ryu practitioner's primary weapon when utilizing the knee as an attacking implement. The most basic, and effective, variation of this technique is a knee strike delivered directly upward into the opponent's groin. However, the goju-ryu stylist can also execute lateral knee strikes to the opponent's

Goju-ryu karate's *tate enpi* elbow strike (1) is a rising blow that can be effectively employed to the opponent's throat. A crane beak eye-gouging technique (2) makes an effective follow-up attack to the elbow strike.

The photo sequence above demonstrates how *goju-ryu* practitioners use their elbows and forearms to block an opponent's elbow strike. In this case, the defender (right) utilizes (1-2) a horizontal elbow/forearm block against his adversary's vertical elbow strike.

knee, outside or inside portion of his thigh, or to a floating rib.

Goju-ryu practitioners can also use the knee as a defensive weapon to block or jam incoming attacks by simply raising their front leg and obstructing the opponent's kick or punch. This defensive maneuver is especially effective against an opponent's front snap kick. To best execute this maneuver, the goju-ryu stylist assumes a "cat stance" (*nekoashi-dachi* in Japanese) and pivots his body, positioning his knee below the opponent's incoming kick. By raising his knee, the goju-ryu practitioner is able to neutralize the attacking leg. The defender can launch an immediate and effective counterattack by kicking his adversary's groin or knee.

*   *   *

For a close-range fighting system such as goju-ryu karate to be effective, practitioners must be skilled at executing knee and elbow techniques. Lateral and vertical elbow strikes are among the most devastating blows a goju-ryu stylist can deliver. Combined with powerful knee strikes, they give the goju-ryu stylist a potent close-quarters combat arsenal that complements nicely the long-range fighting techniques in the system.

The knee can be a devastating weapon, as the sequence above illustrates. Facing (1) an opponent who delivers (2) a hand strike, the *goju-ryu* stylist (left) responds by blocking the blow to the outside while simultaneously counterattacking (3) with a *hiza geri* knee kick to the midsection.

JUJUTSU'S STRIKING TECHNIQUES
Classical Version of the Art Includes Much More Than Chokes, Locks and Throws

by Rory A. Miller • Photos by Rory A. Miller • June 1997

Traditional *jujutsu* styles are among the most well-documented and battle-tested classical martial arts. As the "art of last resort" for Japanese *bushi* (warriors), jujutsu was used on both the battlefield and in duels between members of rival martial arts schools from Japan's medieval period until the Meiji restoration in the late 1800s. Interested more in effect than questions of style, the bushi helped mold the many jujutsu systems into extremely pragmatic fighting arts.

Jujutsu has received a lot of attention in recent years, thanks primarily to its success in the reality combat arena, where a number of practitioners have successfully demonstrated the art's formidable grappling techniques.

Striking to create an opening in the opponent's defenses is probably the best-known method of integrating grappling and striking techniques.

This popular emphasis on throws, locks and choke holds had caused many people to overlook jujutsu's highly effective striking techniques, known as *atemi waza*. Ignoring these potentially devastating strikes in a fight against a jujutsu practitioner could be a fatal oversight.

Types of Jujutsu Strikes

Jujutsu atemi waza are taught with an emphasis on power, target and range. The body mechanics are very similar to those featured in Okinawan karate, in which the hips are used to convey power to a single point, thus magnifying the impact of a strike.

All blows in jujutsu *kata* (training forms) are aimed at the opponent's joints, nerve centers or organs. The most common striking weapons are the edge of the jujutsu stylist's hand, the heel of his palm or an extended-knuckle fist. All jujutsu kicking techniques are delivered low and strong.

Atemi Waza Combinations

Jujutsu is an extremely integrated art. The system's strikes, throws and locks often set one another up or combine in a single, damaging attack.

There are four basic ways in which jujutsu practitioners blend striking and grappling techniques: by immobilizing a target, by creating an opening in the opponent's defenses, by using strikes as throws or by using "two-way action."

When using grappling techniques to immobilize a target, the jujutsu practitioner may merely entangle one or both of the opponent's arms and strike with a knee, his head or his free hand. Or he may choose to use a trick of physics to "freeze" an opponent in place.

In jujutsu's *yukichigai* "assassination" kata, the *tori* (the partner performing the technique) suddenly grabs the wrist of the *uke* (the partner receiving the technique) while walking by him. Properly timed, this maneuver catches the uke in a trianqle formed by his feet and the downward pull on his arm. The tori then pivots around his partner—who cannot move either foot—and delivers a straight *shuto* (knifehand) strike to the uke's seventh cervical vertebra.

The body mechanics used in *jujutsu* striking techniques are similar to those in Okinawan karate, in which the hips help convey power to the strikes. The photo sequence illustrates this point. The jujutsu practitioner halts (1) an opponent's punch with a double knifehand block to the arm and then delivers (2) a right knifehand strike to the neck. The blow clears the way for a follow-up palm-heel strike (3) to the chin, which cocks the jujutsu stylist's hips for a powerful reverse punch (4) to the solar plexus.

Traditional *jujutsu* practitioners often first immobilize an opponent with a grappling technique, paving the way for an uncontested follow-up strike. In the example above, a well-timed tug (1) on the opponent's arm pulls him off-balance and paralyzes his ability to move in any direction he desires. The jujutsu practitioner can safely pivot (2) behind the opponent and deliver a knifehand strike to the back of the neck.

Striking to create an opening in the opponent's defenses is probably the best-known method of integrating grappling and striking techniques. In jujutsu's *taikodachi/nuki uchi* kata, the tori blocks a downward sword slash and punches his partner in the solar plexus with an extended-knuckle punch. Using the uke's involuntary reaction, the tori then pivots and throws his partner to the ground. This kata probably introduced the throw that became judo's *ippon seoi nage* (one-arm shoulder throw).

The traditional jujutsu throws were not the clean, safe techniques seen in modern sport judo. Often, the throw itself was a strike or combination of strikes that had the side effect of leaving the enemy on the ground.

In jujutsu's *michizuri* kata, the tori finishes with the old form of *osoto-gari* (outer reap), driving his heel into the nerve center at the top of his opponent's calf muscle. This blow is, at the very least, painful and will cause the opponent's lower leg to spasm. At the worst, the blow may disarticulate the opponent's knee, causing him to go down—especially when you take into consideration the Y-strike the tori simultaneously delivers with his inside hand to the cricoid cartilage at the lower portion of the opponent's larynx.

A fourth way in which jujutsu stylists can blend grappling and striking techniques is by using "two-way action"—in other words, combining a punch with a pulling maneuver. Very few jujutsu blocks are, in fact, simply blocking techniques. Given the slightest opportunity, the jujutsu stylist's blocking arm will roll and pull, immobilizing the opponent's striking limb, disrupting his balance and creating an opening for a counterstrike.

A devastating example of this two-way action is the final move in the "double elbow" kata. At this point, the jujutsu practitioner has blocked his opponent's low punch into his grip. The finishing strike is an elbow smash delivered to the opponent's face as the jujutsu stylist pulls him into the blow by the trapped hand.

In jujutsu's *yotsugumi/harai obi gaeshi* kata, which is essentially a very old form for wrestling in armor, the tori pulls on the receiver's *obi* (belt) while simultaneously striking the throat with an elbow. The lift-and-pull action on the uke's belt prevents him from moving away while also increasing the damage of the strike. As the tori continues this two-way action, the receiver is bent backward and levered to the ground.

Simultaneous Strikes

Jujutsu stylists' penchant for infighting affords them the opportunity to deliver simultaneous combinations, especially against an opponent who is not comfortable at halitosis range. For example, a ridgehand delivered to

The traditional *kata taikodachi/nuki uchi* includes a striking/grappling combination in which the *jujutsu* practitioner steps inside an attacker's sword strike and blocks (1) the blow while counterattacking with an extended-knuckle fist to the tip of the *xiphoid* process. This maneuver allows the jujutsu stylist to pivot (2) into position for a one-arm shoulder throw.

the back of the opponent's neck with a hooking action can be combined with an elbow strike or spearhand to the throat.

The following sequence appears several times in different kata: the jujutsu practitioner drops into a "horse" stance at the opponent's side and

---

Jujutsu has received a lot of attention in recent years, thanks primarily to its success in the reality combat arena, where a number of practitioners have successfully demonstrated the art's formidable grappling techniques.

---

executes a hook punch with both hands— one to the kidney and one to the bladder. The combined shock waves are very unpleasant for the victim.

Philosophy

Jujutsu evolved as a last-ditch solution for Japanese warriors who had lost their weapons during battle. It was fashioned as a defense for the fighter who was alone, unarmed and unarmored, and facing armed and armored adversaries intent on his death.

True to form and to history, the jujutsu practitioner's fighting range is inside, close to the opponent—the best range to use a sword, kick or most punches. The jujutsu stylist's "kitchen" is inside his opponent's reach, and his atemi waza are designed to possess power and precision at very close range.

Always remember jujutsu's "golden rule": Apply your most powerful weapon to your enemy's most vulnerable point at his time of greatest imbalance.

LEOPARD KUNG FU
Fast, Fierce and Aggressive Techniques Characterize This Shaolin Animal System

by Jane Hallander • Photos by Vern Miller • September 1997

Chinese martial arts are unique in their emphasis on the study of animal habits and fighting tactics. For centuries, kung fu stylists have faithfully imitated the characteristics and habits of birds, snakes, mammals and insects in an effort to recreate the particular essence that makes each creature an efficient fighter within its own domain.

As martial artists saw an opportunity to improve or change their kung fu systems, they often injected the influence and spirit of the animal that inspired the change. The Shaolin kung fu system, in particular, heavily embraced the use of animal techniques and includes five animals in its curriculum.

It all began toward the end of China's Ming dynasty (A.D. 1522-1566) with a martial-artist-turned-Shaolin monk named Gok Yuen, who had been an expert in empty-hand fighting and sword techniques before he became a traveling Buddhist monk. When he joined the Shaolin Temple, he realized that Shaolin kung fu was too external in nature, using too much force against force in its self-defense techniques. He subsequently redesigned the system to create a more balanced structure of external and internal components.

Gok later met a martial artist during his travels named Li Sao, who introduced him to Bak Yuk Fung, another famous martial artist of that era.

Pow chui, the leopard fist (1), is the most common technique in shaolin leopard style kung fu and can be combined (1a) with a grabbing technique to strike an opponent in the neck. The striking surfaces is the second joint of the hand, not the knuckles.

The *hak pow seung shu* technique (1) is a series of four rapid-fire leopard fist strikes delivered (1a) to the opponent's torso and face.

All three men returned to the Shaolin Temple and founded the "five-animal form" (called *ng ying kuen* in Chinese).

The Shaolin system was originally made up of 18 techniques, but Bak increased the number to 128 movements and included five separate animal imitations in the expanded style—leopard, tiger, crane, snake and dragon.

In China, the leopard is considered second only to the tiger in terms of ferocity and power. Although smaller than the tiger, the leopard is stronger for his size and faster. Tigers rely on their size and explosive force to overpower their adversaries. The leopard, on the other hand, is an animal that possesses long, smooth, even-toned muscle tissue within a sleek, fast frame. Leopards depend on lightning-fast speed and footwork rather than on brute strength to overcome their adversaries.

"Leopards are known for their power, but not tense power," explains Vern Miller, a Bremerton, Washington-based kung fu instructor. "Instead, a leopard's power is delivered from loose, relaxed, whiplike movements generated by the animal's great speed."

The Shaolin monks chose the leopard as one of their five animal forms to provide a balance between the strength of the tiger and the quick, penetrating force of the crane. The Shaolin leopard form develops both strength and speed in the practitioner. The Chinese call this kind of speed-driven penetrating strength *lik* or *li*.

The leopard form does little to enhance one's internal power. Because internal power is developed from slow, precise movements designed to generate *chi* (internal energy), the fast, sharp techniques that characterize leopard kung fu have value only as external fighting techniques.

The leopard form's primary fist technique is *pow chui* (leopard fist), which uses penetrating force to produce trauma throughout an opponent's body. Pow chui is formed by folding the fingers forward to the second joint rather than to the knuckle, as with a regular fist. The thumb is held flat along the outside of the fist, adding stability and strength to the configuration. The shape of the leopard fist allows the practitioner to focus power into a small surface area, thereby greatly increasing the overall force and penetration of the punch.

Pow chui is a "spring loaded" technique, often administered with a twisting action of the forearm, which gives the punch a corkscrew appearance. Because of the whiplike speed a leopard practitioner can generate in the blow, the pow chui penetrates through an opponent much the same way a bullet would.

Leopard practitioners must condition their hands to deliver pow chui techniques. The training involves punching sandbags and performing knuckle push-ups to strengthen the hands. If the leopard stylist doesn't condition his fist properly before executing pow chui strikes, he could break his knuckles.

The Shaolin leopard system includes a fist technique (1) that is actually a downward forearm strike delivered (1a) to the opponent's throat or face.

The leopard practitioner must also condition his hands and wrists if he wishes to safely withstand the force of a properly executed pow chui. To accomplish this, he can hold a rubber ball with both hands and squeeze it with all of his strength 100 times each day.

The Shaolin leopard form also includes a regular fist technique that appears in several forearm and elbow strikes. Leopards are adept at transferring external power (*ging*) to the area of their bodies that makes contact with another animal, and their kung fu counterparts are no different when it comes to dealing with a human adversary. For leopard forearm and elbow strikes, power is released only at the point of contact, producing strong, penetrating force.

There are few blocking or defensive movements in the leopard practitioner's repertoire, illustrating the advanced nature of the style. Rather than block first and then counterstrike, the leopard practitioner will deflect an oncoming blow with the forearm of his own punch. As he deflects the strike, he changes the angle of his punch slightly to find the opponent's weak area.

This type of simultaneous offense and defense is useless without quick, active footwork that allows the leopard practitioner to keep driving forward into his opponent. As he deflects and strikes the opponent with his forearm and fist, the leopard practitioner times his footwork to coordinate with his hand techniques. This timing can be honed by practicing leopard techniques with a partner.

Leopard footwork features quick, short postures designed to stabilize the kung fu stylist and produce strong, mobile stances. Because speed must be backed by stability, leopard practitioners utilize the square "horse riding" stance or the "bow and arrow" stance while stationary. When moving, they employ shifting and twisting footwork to quickly close in on the opponent or alter his angle of attack.

Following are several other techniques that characterize the leopard:

• *Hak pow seung shu* (black panther climbs the tree)—This technique, which illustrates the speed and aggressiveness of the leopard's attack, is a rapid-fire series of four leopard fists delivered to the opponent's face and torso before he can react. Because stability is necessary for the correct focus of power in this technique, a square stance is the footwork of preference.

• *Gum pow hay kau* (golden leopard plays ball)—This maneuver, which is a combination of leopard hand techniques and footwork, features a regular closed punch, called *kup chui*, that strikes down on the opponent's head, much

The *pow li ding sun* technique (1) is a simultaneous double fist strike delivered (1a) to the temples of two different opponents.

like the action of bouncing a ball. As the leopard practitioner strikes with kup chui, he also delivers a low cross kick to the opponent's groin.

• *Pow li ding sun* **(leopard steadies his body)**—This leopard technique can be either defensive or offensive in nature. When used defensively, it is a double upward block performed from a square horse stance. When employed in an offensive manner, pow li ding sun becomes a simultaneous double fist attack to the opponent's temple.

Leopard techniques are first practiced slowly and with good definition so that students learn them properly. Otherwise, the movements will be fast, sloppy techniques that lack focus and power. Speed comes naturally after students familiarize themselves with the correct form and application of each technique.

As they develop speed and precision in their techniques, students must also work on assuming the aggressive, fierce spirit of the leopard. Once they have captured the animal's spirit, they are well on their way to "becoming" the leopard—a level achieved by only the most advanced Shaolin kung fu practitioners.

OPEN-HAND THRUSTS AND STRIKES
Are They the Ultimate Tools for Self-Defense?

by Mike Soohey • Photos by Todd Musselman • March 1998

Most martial artists are accustomed to using straight and arcing punches when they want a powerful strike. However, there is another classification of extremely effective hand techniques: open-hand thrusts and strikes.

These techniques can be best put into action by first understanding what separates a thrust from a strike. The major differences exist in the delivery and positioning of the fingers and knuckles as contact is made.

A thrust and strike differ from a standard punch in that the blow is delivered with an open hand rather than a closed fist. A thrust is thrown along a straight line, while a strike follows a curved path.

Two techniques that highlight these differences are the spearhand and chicken-beak attacks. The spearhand thrust is directed along a straight line with the hand and fingers held straight out in a rigid fashion. The chicken-beak strike traces an arc and positions all five fingertips together to form a point.

By ripping at an attacker's face and sinking the nails into the flesh, [women] can stop an assailant long enough to escape or counter with another technique.

The techniques that fit into the thrust and strike classifications are formidable attacks that offer variety, deceptiveness and strength. Of course, to develop them into usable weapons takes consistent practice and conditioning.

Spearhand Thrust

Perhaps the most popular open-hand technique is the spearhand thrust. Although basic in application, this puncturing blow takes a lot of time and repetitions to hone. This is because the tips of the fingers make the contact, and this relatively delicate region must be carefully conditioned and developed.

To make a spearhand thrust, extend your fingers straight out and bend your thumb inward against your palm. It's important to keep your attacking hand rigid and all four fingers together. While the main area of contact is the tips of the three middle fingers, the little finger helps hold these digits

The spearhand thrust is an effective self-defense technique that can be used to attack soft targets like the neck. Mike Soohey (left) demonstrates on opponent Nick Sokolsky.

together and elevates the overall driving force behind the blow.

The spearhand thrust is designed to be performed with the fingers straight or slightly flexed. While the latter method helps prevent finger injury, the position you choose depends on your level of hand strength and conditioning. In either case, it's imperative to thrust your fingers into and beyond your target zone and retract them quickly. An excellent drill is to thrust your hand into an imaginary target while pulling your lead arm back until it rests under the elbow of the attacking hand. This snapping back of the nonhitting hand increases the power of the thrust.

There are two primary ways to deliver a spearhand thrust. If performed with the hand held in a vertical position, where the thumb is placed on top, it is effective for attacking the solar plexus or penetrating inner organs such as the kidney and spleen. If performed with the hand held horizontally, where the palm faces up or down, it is perfect for attacking between or just under the floating ribs. In a life-or-death situation, it can even target an adversary's throat or eyes.

You can improve the vertical and horizontal variations of the spearhand by shoving your hand into a large bowl of coarse sand or a *makiwara* board. This will strengthen the thrusting motion and toughen the fingers and knuckles.

One-Finger Thrust

The one-finger spearhand thrust is an offshoot of the classical spearhand. Also referred to as the finger jab, this technique is performed by

If you are looking to attack both your opponent's eyes at the same time, try the two-finger thrust. It can temporarily blind your attacker and give you time to finish him off or escape.

extending only the forefinger; all the other fingers remain clenched. The one-finger thrust can attack small, vulnerable areas such as the eyes, throat and solar plexus.

With only one finger involved, the thrusting action must be pinpoint accurate. The stronger and better conditioned your forefinger is, the more control and accuracy you'll have. A weak forefinger can easily be injured. For this reason, you should devote extra time to conditioning it by thrusting it repeatedly into coarse sand.

The one-finger thrust can be delivered by turning the back of your hand up or out. Turning the hand up usually helps you flick the weapon into your opponent's eyes or throat. The quick delivery simulates the straight-line approach used in fencing. If you use the technique to attack the solar plexus, you may want to turn your hand out. This will allow a greater power surge as you make contact.

Two-Finger Thrust

In the two-finger spearhand thrust, the forefinger and middle finger are extended to form a "V" shape. The other fingers are clenched, and the thumb holds them down. Your palm faces downward.

The technique is especially effective for attacking the eyes because the "V" shape allows it to simultaneously target both of them. The luxury of the blow is that it gives you two chances to hit your target, and the quick flicking delivery allows very little time for an opponent to defend against it.

When executing the two-finger thrust, it's important to keep both fingers rigid to maximize power. This also helps you avoid getting them bruised or broken.

Sword-Peak Hand

One of the most vicious thrusting techniques is the sword-peak hand, also known as the tiger-mouth thrust. It's a powerful attack that targets your adversary's throat. To perform it, you extend your thrusting hand with the palm down. Position your fingers so they are extended and firmly placed against one another. The thumb should be held apart from the fingers.

A common application is to thrust the sword-peak hand into an opponent's neck, hitting with the curved area between the thumb and the forefinger. The scissorlike attack is a stunning blow that can cause severe damage to the front of the neck. With the potential severity of the thrust, it should be used only on the street. The technique also gives you the option

The sword-peak hand uses the flesh between the thumb and forefinger to strike a target such as the neck. Because it can result in severe injury, its use should be reserved for real self-defense situations.

to grab the throat and follow with a punch, knee blast or sweep.

When using the sword-peak hand, the "web" area between the thumb and forefinger can act as a catcher's mitt for an incoming punch. As this soft area absorbs the impact of a punch, it also allows you to grab the fist. This can put you in position to nullify any subsequent attack made with that hand. Then you can quickly counter with a punch, kick or throw of your own.

Ripping-Hand Thrust

The ripping-hand thrust can be classified as a fingertip-thrusting technique because it uses the fingertips to rip at a specific target. The technique is easily performed by curling all four fingers and the thumb toward the palm. Don't curl them too far or they will not be able to make contact with the target. Just enough curvature ensures that the fingertips will point outward and rip into vulnerable targets such as the face, neck and groin.

The sole intent of using this technique is to maim an aggressive assailant who wants to hurt you. Women with long, sharp fingernails can use them to their advantage: By ripping at an attacker's face and sinking the nails into the flesh, they can stop an assailant long enough to escape or counter with another technique.

Hitting the makiwara board can develop the ripping-hand thrust. Advanced practitioners sometimes condition their fingertips by hitting a brick wall.

Palm-Heel Thrust

The palm heel can be used in several attacking and blocking variations. When used in either mode, it can be turned into a thrusting or striking attack. The final choice of which to use depends on the direction in which you launch the attack or block: forward, upward, downward or hooking.

The forward palm-heel technique is classified as a thrust. It is executed by holding your hand open and bent back at the wrist. The fingers are curved away from the palm. Some practitioners like to keep their fingers tightly pressed together, while others prefer to separate them. In either case, it's essential to tense all of them as you make contact. The same for the thumb: You can press it against the side of the palm or hold it separate. Impact is made with the heel of the palm.

The thrust can attack such targets as the temple, solar plexus, rib cage, stomach and kidneys. Practitioners who master this technique can knock an opponent unconscious with a solid shot to the face, head or chin. It can also be used as a devastating follow-up after a punch or kick to the body.

While this blow offers many offensive possibilities, it's availability as a block should not be overlooked. It can be a powerful weapon for smashing or deflecting kicks and punches. When blocking a jab or a rear cross, the technique acts like a catcher's mitt as its padded heel surface diminishes the force of the blow. Even against a strong arcing punch such as a hook or uppercut, the palm heel can be used to deflect the blow and render it harmless.

When executing the straightforward variation, you can summon extra power by first cocking the heel of your attacking hand at your waist. As you attack, snap your wrist back and thrust out with your palm facing forward. This technique can also be performed by pointing the outer edge of the hand downward to effect a side delivery aimed at the torso.

Palm-Heel Strike

The upward, downward and hooking palm-heel techniques are classified as strikes because they travel in a vertical or horizontal arc. The upward palm-heel strike closely resembles an uppercut because it moves along a similar path. It can be used to smash upward against an opponent's chin or nose, or to pummel the temple or solar plexus.

To build striking power, begin this technique by positioning your attacking hand near your kidney area with the palm facing up at an angle. When stepping forward with your rear leg, simultaneously swing your palm up toward the target. As your palm traces a vertical arc, it will turn over and

The upward palm-heel strike follows the same path as an uppercut punch. The best targets include the chin, nose and solar plexus.

161

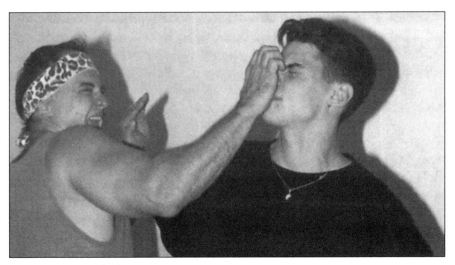

The bear-hand strike mimics the paw motion of the ursine mammal. It can be used to swat at an opponent with the palm or to rip at his face with the claws.

face upward as you make contact and follow through. Your rear leg will set down in front of you as you twist your attacking arm upward. Keep your elbow slightly bent and your shoulders open as you strike.

The downward palm-heel strike is cocked at a high point before it is launched in an inward and descending manner toward a low target. You should swing the striking hand in a snapping motion to generate force. Your wrist should be bent back as you make contact. This blow follows a downward vertical arc into the solar plexus or front abdominal area. If you are taller than your opponent, the technique can be aimed at the face or chin.

This type of strike can also be used as a push when a charging assailant attempts to tackle you. You can then strike him and push him away while you get set for a follow-up technique.

The hooking palm-heel strike follows a horizontal arc to its target. Like a classical hook punch, it can be used to pummel the body, especially the rib cage. If used on the temple and jaw, the palm heel provides some protection against injuring your hand.

When using any of the three variations, keep your wrist cocked back as you make contact or you may end up hitting the target with your fingers or the top of the palm. While the resulting slap can be painful, it lacks the punishing force of the palm heel.

The technique can be used with the lead arm in an attacking or blocking mode, but stepping forward as you strike with your rear hand can be more effective. From a fighting stance or side stance, you can advance with the attacking hand cocked alongside your waist or behind your shoulder. Then, as you swing that hand in a horizontal arc, your arm will be forward and your elbow bent as you make contact.

Other Useful Strikes

Like a pecking fowl, the chicken-beak strike attacks an adversary's vulnerable regions, including the eyes, throat, groin and armpits. This unusual but effective technique is executed by first pressing the fingers and thumb together to form a compact striking point. The hand position corresponds to a bird's beak and can be used to attack downward, forward or horizontally. Conditioned and callused fingertips, as well as long fingernails, can make the technique more effective.

The bear-hand strike is an open-hand technique in which the second knuckles of all four fingers are used to attack. The thumb should be tightly folded into the palm. This half-clenched fist can be a powerful striking or ripping weapon that targets the face. It's a brutal self-defense technique capable of maiming or even knocking out an adversary.

HSING-I CHUAN'S FIVE-ELEMENT BOXING
The Exploding Fists of China's "Other" Internal Art
by Keith Boggess • Photos by Keith Boggess • July 1998

The mind possesses tremendous power. Physical strength can move heavy objects and even smash irritating things, but much more power is generated when that physical strength unites with the mind's intention. We hear how a middle-aged lady lifts an overturned car off her child, or how a man carries a heavy safe filled with valuables out of a burning house. Those superhuman feats, many of which have been reliably documented, tempt us with a glimpse of the untapped potential of a unified body and mind.

Hsing-i chuan, one of China's three major internal arts, means "mind and will boxing." It coordinates physical power with mental intention. Although many martial artists equate internal with soft, they might be surprised to learn that unlike *tai chi chuan* and *pa kua chang*, China's other popular internal arts, hsing-i is linear and explosive.

Despite the simplicity, each strike of five-element boxing is difficult to master, and just one method can be used almost as a complete self-defense system.

At the beginning levels, hsing-i exhibits power and tension visibly so the student's attacking energy (or *fa jing*) and body strength are developed. Only much later will the movements take on latent strength, appearing soft yet remaining strong within. At the highest level, those two energies—the external and the internal—merge in dynamic motion. The various movements then become like a long river, sometimes flowing tranquilly and sometimes torrentially.

Two Faces

Hsing-i's movements can be categorized into two substyles: five-element boxing and 12-animal boxing. The five-element fists, which serve as the fundamentals of the art, are single moves known as the "splitting fist," "drilling fist," "punching fist," "pounding fist" and "crossing fist." Ordinarily, the 12-animal styles are the dragon, tiger, cock, alligator, swallow, sparrow hawk, horse, monkey, *tai* (phoenix), snake, eagle and bear, but regional styles may use a slightly different set. Most of the forms are short, with many consisting of only one move. However, practitioners can repeat the movements as long as they desire, especially with the five-element fists.

Five-element boxing is the essence of the art. When tournaments come, hsing-i competitors often train by practicing nothing but the five fists. Each move is that important. Consequently, many past Chinese masters practiced only the five fists and nothing else, and some even specialized in only one or two. Each move is that powerful.

As the names of the fists imply, each represents one of the five traditional elements in Chinese metaphysics. The splitting fist represents metal (gold), the drilling fist stands for water, the punching fist denotes wood, the pounding fist symbolizes fire and the crossing fist represents earth. Furthermore, practicing the fist methods mirrors the two popular five-element cycles found in Asian philosophy and traditional Chinese medicine: creation and destruction.

In practice, each fist leads to the next one in the creation cycle. Because metal creates water, the splitting fist is practiced first, and the drilling fist follows it. Water creates wood, so the punching fist is done after the drilling fist. Because wood creates fire, the cannon fist is performed after the punching fist. Finally, fire creates earth, so the crossing fist is done last. Then the cycle starts again.

Likewise, each fist philosophically overcomes the other according to the order of the destructive cycle. Metal destroys wood in the way that an ax can split a tree, so the splitting fist suppresses the punching fist. Wood destroys earth in the way that a wooden structure can hold back dirt, so the punching fist overcomes the crossing fist. Earth suppresses water in the way that a dam can control a river, so the crossing fist overcomes the drilling fist. Water destroys fire in the way that a bucket of water can douse a flame, so the drilling fist overcomes the pounding fist. Fire destroys metal in the way that heat can melt metal, so the pounding fist overcomes the splitting fist. And the cycle continues.

Despite the simplicity, each strike of five-element boxing is difficult to master, and just one method can be used almost as a complete self-defense system. Although the techniques may include up to three moves, each can be applied in numerous combat situations.

Three Gems

The splitting fist provides an excellent example of how one move has many applications. As a metal element, it carries the image of an ax chopping wood. An ax usually has a dull side, shaped like a hammer, as well as an edge. Likewise, the splitting fist has two parts—a fist strike, which can

Against any forward motion—a punch, in this case—the *hsing-i* practitioner (right) presses the opponent's arm downward with her lead hand (1) and circles her other arm up to claw his face (2).

be compared to the hammering blow, and a chop. The technique teaches three important skills: the spiral fist, the chop and the critical three-in-one stance. Mastering these helps the student develop a good foundation for the rest of the art.

First is the basic three-in-one stance. Physically, the term means that the three sections of the body—the legs, torso and head—coordinate as one. Metaphysically, it means that the three sections of the universe—heaven, earth and man— unite through this posture. The boxer masters the stance through a "stake" exercise, in which he sits in the stance correctly, with his hands, chest and feet concave, for a specified period of time. This conditions the body and develops the circulation of *chi*, or vital energy.

True internal power comes from storing energy and exerting it explosively along a spiral path.

Therefore, the back needs to be straight, the butt tucked in and the tongue lightly touching the top of the mouth.

A form of *chi kung*, the posture helps gather the chi and open the meridians. The boxer circulates energy through coordinating his breath with his visual intent. On the inhalation, energy is visualized going into the body through the center of the lead palm. In that area is an acupuncture point (pericardium 6) that works as one of the five main gates through which chi enters the body. The upper body is relaxed as the practitioner accumulates energy in the *tan tien* (point below the navel). After some skill has been acquired, the chi can be visualized coming through the tips of the fingers,

As she steps forward again, the hsing-i stylist uses a spiral fist to jam the attack and force the opponent back (3). She continues by pressing one of the attacker's arms and hitting his chest with her palm (4).

an important area where hsing-i students often concentrate power.

Second is the spiral fist. Returning to the ax metaphor, it is the spiral fist that creates the crack for the final split. The fist, however, is not the normal fist of most boxing schools. The weapon is made by first forming a tight fist and then twisting it as if holding a rope. That way, it can be drilled into targets such as the opponent's throat.

The spiral fist can also be used in a regular punch, specifically when performing the punching fist. When a normal fist is made and the fingers are tightened to form the spiral fist, the first knuckle becomes the point of contact for striking the soft areas of the torso. The whole arm tenses for this powerful technique.

Third is the chop. It is formed by making the palm concave and facing it forward. The hand angles slightly out so the palm heel can strike the chest or the fingers can claw the face. The chop is usually set up by the fist attack, in which the spiral fist beats the opponent back for the split—much the same way the dull part of the ax forces a wedge into a log. When the chop comes, it penetrates the "crack" made by the hammering blow and strikes the opponent.

Details

To perform the splitting fist, the boxer first assumes the three-in-one stance. From there, he tightens his hands into fists and pulls the lead one down in a circular motion to the center of his body, rubbing it tightly against his chest as he moves the arm up his centerline. He raises it to his chin and thrusts it straight out with the heart of the fist, or the palm side, facing up and the first knuckles forming a straight line with his nose. His other hand is kept near his tan tien.

From there, the boxer continues with the chop. He brings his rear fist up his centerline to his chin and thrusts his hand in front of his face in an arc. As the fist reaches the arc's end, he opens it to effect a palm strike, relying on the palm heel's pinkie side to strike the target. Through all movements, the boxer keeps his arms moving in a circular pattern.

Those moves teach principles with which anyone can defend himself in a variety of situations. They show how the arms protect the centerline while they occupy the opponent's limbs. Also, they show how the elbows protect the chest and the hands protect the heart.

Applications

In addition to these principles, the moves have specific applications. The fist attack can be used against an opponent who has extended his lead arm. By stepping forward quickly, the boxer can grab the other man's wrist and pull him off-balance. As he falls forward, the defender can continue the motion and strike his throat with the spiral fist.

Also, the spiral fist can be used against a wrist or arm grab. By bringing his other hand down forcefully against the opponent's grabbing limb while

Physical strength can move heavy objects and even smash irritating things, but much more power is generated when that physical strength unites with the mind's intention.

shooting his trapped arm up the centerline to twist against the weak part of the opponent's grip, the hsing-i boxer can release the grab. Then he can continue the circling motion with his previously trapped arm and attack the throat with a spiral fist. If the opponent is too far away, the boxer can step forward and attack.

The chopping motion can also defend against a variety of frontal attacks. Against any forward motion—such as a punch, push or grab—the defender can press the opponent's arm with his lead hand and circle his other arm up and out to claw at his face. Because the motions are circular and on the centerline, it takes only a moment to execute them.

By stepping forward, both motions of the splitting fist can be executed as one attack. The defender steps quickly and strongly into the opponent's attack. The spiral fist jams the attack and, along with pressure from the stepping leg, forces the opponent back. The defender continues by pressing one of the attacker's arms and hitting his chest with his palm.

The other four elemental boxing methods are just as applicable as the splitting fist. In fact, each one teaches a powerful technique and a strategy to use in fighting. The first one uses a pressing motion and a follow-up attack. The drilling fist uses that same principle, but the pressing hand receives the attack with wrapping energy and counters with a drilling fist. The third one, the punching fist, teaches taking the initiative and countering directly and swiftly. The pounding fist teaches defending with one hand while countering with the other. The last one, the crossing fist, teaches defending and attacking with the same motion and countering an attack from an angle.

Naturally, mastering five-element boxing requires much study. Although the moves are few, developing the proper power demands consistent practice. You can learn the forms correctly but still lack the power. True internal power comes from storing energy and exerting it explosively along a spiral path. Hsing-i's energy release, unlike karate's, causes the shoulders and waist to be turned into the opponent. Because of that, the body must be kept agile.

In its youth, hsing-i chuan began as a totally new approach to traditional Shaolin boxing. By emphasizing the centerline and the need to master only a few moves, the art became a jewel in the classical Chinese martial arts. Today it exists as an example of how the passage of centuries strengthens the most effective styles. The serious martial artist will recognize those arts that have passed the test of time as the wonderful cultural treasures they are.

WHIPPING HANDS OF LIMA LAMA
by Rodney Ley • Photos by Rodney Ley • May 1999

If the martial art of *lima lama* were a human being, it would be diagnosed with a split personality. One minute it's graceful and smooth, and the next minute it's deceptive and deadly.

That's precisely why some 200,000 practitioners around the world have taken to the art like Sybil to a therapist's couch.

Possibly the single most changeable part of lima lama is its hand techniques. Said to compose some 60 percent of the style's repertoire, they can morph from the fluttering appendages of a hula dancer into the weapons of an empty-hand warrior in the blink of an eye.

Beginnings

Roughly translated, lima lama means the "hand of wisdom." That wisdom originated on the South Pacific island of Samoa, where the style sprouted from a blending of the traditional movements of Polynesian dancers and the battle-proven methods of the fiercest warriors. That dichotomy led to what has become one of lima lama's defining characteristics: a kick-butt effectiveness disguised as a graceful and beautiful art.

Samoan Tino Tuiolosega systematized the art's techniques in the early 1960s, after which they spread to neighboring islands in the South Pacific, including Hawaii. Tuiolosega introduced the style to California in 1964. One of lima lama's best-known American practitioners is Ted Tabura, a Hawaiian transplant who now lives in Gardena, California. After having cut his teeth in *kajukenbo* and *Okinawa-te*, Tabura received his introduction to lima lama in 1967 from the late John Louise, a direct student of Tuiolosega. Tabura now spreads the word about the Polynesian art whenever the opportunity arises at tournaments and seminars around the world.

Discovering the Softer Side

When Tabura began learning lima lama, he says, it was difficult for him to switch from the hard styles he had studied to the soft style from the South Pacific. That's an affliction that frequently befalls martial artists who change arts.

Tabura says that lima lama is characterized as a soft style because of its many flowing open-hand movements derived from Polynesian dances. However, when an opponent fully commits himself to an attack and unwittingly leaves an opening for a lima lama stylist to counter, the art leans toward what Tabura classifies as "medium-hard." Under those conditions, punches and

THE WHIPPING TECHNIQUE: The opponent grabs Ted Tabura's neck with his right hand (1). Tabura snaps up his left arm and strikes his opponent's face (2). The opponent counters with a left punch, which Tabura blocks (3). The *lima lama* stylist then delivers a strike to his opponent's throat (4). Next, he seizes his opponent's right arm (5) and locks it (6). To finish, Tabura pivots counterclockwise (7) and uses his swinging left arm to send his opponent to the ground (8).

elbow strikes to the head may be used to subdue a resisting opponent.

Hand techniques occupy a very important position in the lima lama repertoire, Tabura says. When they are done correctly, they look almost effortless. This has led many to notice what has been called its nonchalant approach to self-defense: Lima lama can be pretty to watch, but the main emphasis is to stop an aggressive assailant—by dislocating his joints if need be.

At times the exotic, flowing nature of lima lama's hand techniques has caused observers to question the art's effectiveness. Tabura, however, harbors no such doubts. While working as a bouncer in a Southern California nightclub, Tabura was forced to use his skills to restrain aggressive and intoxicated customers. Each time he used one of the art's hand techniques, he was reassured of the effectiveness of lima lama and of the wisdom of its founders.

Numerous martial artists have claimed that the more flowery an art looks, the longer it takes for a student to master its techniques to the point at which they can be used in real self-defense situations. Does this same caveat apply to lima lama? Tabura says it took him four years to become proficient in the art, which includes hundreds of techniques. "It took me six months just to learn two moves due to my background with exclusively hard styles," he says.

However, once a person puts in his time and masters lima lama—its hand techniques in particular—the hard work will pay off in the form of real-world self-defense proficiency, Tabura says.

Hands That Flow

Perhaps the most effective set of techniques within the lima lama system is the one known as "whipping hands." They are grouped together because they rely on the concept of flowing—each technique smoothly follows the one before it with such a seamless transition that the whole kit and caboodle appears to be a single movement.

"The whipping-hand [techniques] use primarily the back hand of your hands, your palms and your fingertips," Tabura says. "They are very much controlled from the inner strength, or *ki*. At the point of impact, you whip [your hand] and then bring it back [to your body]. It's a flowing motion, like the hula [dance], but it is executed very quickly, like getting slapped on the face. Using the palm or the whole hand, the power at the point of impact after you deliver the punch [allows it to] become a devastating hit."

The remainder of this article will discuss three whipping-hand techniques extracted from the lima lama system. Although each is intended as a response to a different attack, all three employ many of the same concepts. "Every technique has many variations," Tabura says. "Whipping hands has hundreds [of variations]. The movements are devastating enough to dislocate a jaw or a shoulder or other body part, and this is a very important weapon of lima lama."

Technique No. 1

The first lima lama whipping-hand technique is called, naturally enough, the whipping technique. It was designed as a response to an opponent who tries to control you by grabbing your neck or collar.

When the opponent reaches out with his right hand and latches on, you respond by snapping your left arm upward and striking his face with the back of your open hand. At this point, he will probably strike back at you out of anger, most likely with a left punch. When he does, you parry his attack with your left hand and drive a right hand strike into his throat. In most instances, this will be sufficient to knock him down.

If you decide that the opponent must be restrained further, you can grab his right wrist as he drops to his knees. Then you pivot clockwise to straighten his arm and apply downward pressure on his elbow to dislocate it. To disorient him further, you can maneuver until your left arm can be driven forcefully against his face and nose. By pivoting counterclockwise and maintaining your hold on his right arm, you can then use your left arm to shove him backward and take him down.

If the opponent is still resisting and attempts to stand up, you can apply a neck lock or pummel his face with an open-hand technique or elbow strike. But in most cases, the attack will have been terminated right after the takedown.

Technique No. 2

The second technique is called *lua ku-u lima*. It was designed to deal with an opponent who commits himself to taking you down using the type of tackle you would see in football.

As soon as the opponent charges in and wraps his arms around your waist, you drop a right elbow strike onto his left shoulder area and a left elbow strike onto his right shoulder area. Don't be concerned if you happen to whack the back of his neck by mistake.

At this point, the opponent will probably try to remain on his feet by clinging to your clothing. You can force him to stand upright by strategically

THE LUA KU-U LIMA TECHNIQUE: The opponent charges in to tackle Ted Tabura (1-2). Tabura raises his arms and then delivers a right elbow strike to his opponent's left shoulder (3) and a left elbow strike to his right shoulder (4). He then uses his right arm to force the bent-over opponent to stand upright (5). Next, Tabura executes a right elbow strike to his opponent's face (6), sending him tumbling to the ground (7).

placing your straightened right arm under his chin and lifting forcefully. Once he is upright, you can use your right elbow to strike his face. That should knock him to the ground.

The opponent will probably not be able to counter your final strike because of the effect of the previous blows and the impact with the ground. But if he manages to put up additional resistance, you can finish him off with strikes to the head.

Technique No. 3

The third technique is called *lua lima*. It was also intended as a response to an opponent who attempts to tackle you, but this time he is approaching you from the side.

Your first step is to quickly free yourself from his grasp by elbow-striking his head. Then you deliver a left palm strike to the back of his neck. Next, you pivot clockwise until you are in position to deliver a right forearm strike to his face. This blow will likely cause him to begin falling backward. As he goes down, you strike the side of his head with the knife edge of your right forearm.

Even before the opponent hits the ground, you should prepare yourself for his possible counterattack. Such a response on his part is unlikely because of the damage inflicted by your previous blows, but you should always be ready.

Tip of the Iceberg

These three self-defense sequences are but the tip of the iceberg of the lima lama system. However, they do offer a quick glimpse of the flowing effectiveness with which the art deals with aggression. Seek out a qualified instructor for more information.

BEWARE THE SERPENT!
Snake Strikes of *Choy Li Fut* Kung Fu
by Jane Hallander • Photos by Don Tittle • September 1999

It was during the Tang dynasty (617-960) that the martial arts really began to flourish in China. Because of the Middle Kingdom's increased interaction with the regions beyond its borders, its fighting arts were spread far and wide, and they are believed to have influenced numerous combat systems practiced in Korea, Okinawa, Vietnam and other nations. This expanded interest in the martial arts brought with it the accelerated development of open-hand fighting styles that involved internal-training methods and pressure-point strikes. In particular, the monks of Shaolin Temple—some of whom were proficient fighters before joining the monastery—became renowned for their prowess at open-hand combat. An important part of their curriculum was snake strikes.

Cult of the Snake

Historically, Asian cultures have viewed the snake quite differently than have Occidental cultures. Partly because Asians were not exposed to Christianity's account of the Garden of Eden, they did not develop the same loathing for members of the ophidian order that Westerners still seem to have. Hence, citizens of China, Korea and Japan were never hesitant about treating themselves to the culinary delights and rejuvenating properties of snakes and snake byproducts.

Chinese martial artists also paid attention to their scaly reptilian friends.

Using techniques from *choy li fut* kung fu's snake form, Nathan Fisher (left) redirects a right-hand punch (1) and a left-hand punch (2) with the art's anchor-hand technique.

Oftentimes, snake handlers and trappers were expert martial artists, and they frequently studied their quarry to see how each species killed its prey and avoided the attacks of predators.

That impromptu field research led to one of the more interesting martial arts developments of the Tang dynasty: the Shaolin snake style, or *se ying*. It evolved as a set of open-hand techniques that target the enemy's vital points: temples, eyes, throat, solar plexus, armpits and groin. So popular were snake strikes that at least one Chinese art, *choy li fut* kung fu, would eventually adopt the serpent tactics and attitudes for one of its advanced internal forms—named, appropriately enough, the snake form.

Power of the Snake

Nathan Fisher, a San Diego-based choy li fut instructor and the head of five White Dragon Martial Arts schools, considers the snake form to be one of the more important concepts in choy li fut. "All the movements in se ying are open-hand techniques," he says. "The power is soft and flowing, designed to penetrate continuously into pressure points. It's a fighting concept that anyone can use successfully, whether they are man or woman, young or old."

Choy li fut's snake form closely mimics the serpent's essence and movements. For instance, an angry cobra coils itself before it attacks. From that position, it straightens its body with devastating speed and accuracy, lashing out to strike its prey. Although it is able to generate a great deal of force from this action, at no time does the cobra pit its strength against that of a larger adversary.

He then roots himself in a horse stance and delivers a spear-palm technique to the throat (3). He finishes with a stab to a pressure point located along the inner thigh (4).

177

Nathan Fisher (left) redirects a shove by splitting the opponent's attack with a double anchor-hand technique from *choy li fut* kung fu (1). Fisher then stops a left-leg kick with a downward defensive slapping technique (2) and shuffles forward to counterattack with a spear-palm technique to the eyes (3).

Another advantage the snake enjoys—one that is perhaps even more important than its unique striking technique—is its ability to develop and release *chi* (internal energy) every time it strikes. It cultivates the same chi that martial artists strive to control so they can execute their techniques with superior focus and penetration. Because the snake is normally calm and relaxed, it possesses more chi than most other animals. When that internal energy is augmented with proper striking technique, it produces a formidable and powerful blow. A similar combination was responsible for the Shaolin monks' most superhuman ability to fight, and those same tactics eventually became part of choy li fut.

Anatomy of the Snake

The serpentine side of choy li fut differs from other animal styles of kung fu because of the relaxed, almost floating way in which the practitioner moves and the hard and soft ways in which he delivers power. Most animal styles teach students to use a tense, aggressive force to strike down an adversary. For instance, the tiger style relies on strictly external strength, and practitioners are noisy and active—with some even producing loud sounds to add force to blows.

In contrast, the snake's energy is quiet and internal. The practitioner

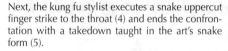

Next, the kung fu stylist executes a snake uppercut finger strike to the throat (4) and ends the confrontation with a takedown taught in the art's snake form (5).

makes no sound as he maneuvers with fluid footwork and administers a soft, penetrating blow. Fist strikes are not used in the style; instead, penetrating palm and fingertip attacks are emphasized. Because blocks and strikes are made simultaneously, there is no difference between defense and offense. One can become the other in a heartbeat. For example, a coiled or circular snake technique can be a defensive beginning that changes into a straight offensive strike. During this transformation, smoothness is more important than speed.

Choy li fut includes several types of fingertip strikes within its repertoire of snake techniques. One of them requires the practitioner to recreate the animal's tongue by extending his index and middle fingers while folding back the others. Called "snake throws out its tongue," the technique usually targets the opponent's vital points.

Another choy li fut fingertip strike involves placing all four fingers together to form an attacking surface that resembles a cobra's head. The practitioner extends his arm to attack in much the same way a cobra strikes at its prey by extending its coiled body. Called *gin ji*, or spear-palm technique, it is an upper block that easily converts into a deadly blow.

The serpentine side of choy li fut differs from other animal styles of kung fu because of the relaxed, almost floating way in which the practitioner moves and the hard and soft ways in which he delivers power.

The choy li fut snake form includes a unique feature called "anchor hand." A combination of a blocking technique and a hooking or grabbing hand movement, it relies on "sticking energy" to trap and control the opponent's striking arm.

In addition to imitating the snake's fighting techniques, kung fu practitioners strive to duplicate the snake's attitude. "An animal's fighting habits are based upon its instinctive nature," Fisher says, "and it's important to preserve that nature in the martial form."

Therefore, it's essential for martial artists who practice the snake form to keep their body supple and in motion at all times. Because the form uses both hard and soft power, they must be able to deliver soft, circular force with their arms and hard, external power with their hands. The key to cultivating this ability lies in developing flexible and relaxed waist action, Fisher says.

Benefits of the Snake

The most important contribution the choy li fut snake form makes to a martial artist's development has to do with chi. Chi flows naturally from a relaxed and concentrated body. Relaxation contributes to softness and flexibility, and concentration leads to calmness and clear thinking. Those attributes will prove useful to any martial artist.

When snake stylists work to develop their chi, they imitate the relaxed posture of the snake and learn to generate internal energy with every movement. To help them relax, they practice the form slowly. Soon, each portion of their body is connected by internal energy. Chi moves through their arms and out to their fingertips, where it becomes a penetrating force. When they are not touching their opponent, they appear to possess no strength at all, but their soft touch becomes a magical sting as soon as it connects with a foe.

Although the snake form may look soft, in an actual fighting situation the actions are speedy and the strikes forceful. On contact, the practitioner's normal energy reserves can be amplified up to seven times.

But the benefits of practicing the snake strikes of choy li fut are more than physical. A snake possesses a special spirit, Fisher says. "If snake stylists cultivate their chi properly, they will be calm enough to mentally look inside their body, feeling peaceful and quiet. Very little of an external nature bothers them," he says. "When they develop the proper snake spirit, they can feel the energy flow from their spine through their arms and out their fingertips."

That quality allows choy li fut practitioners to move calmly and deliberately before they strike or block. As soon as they decide to take action, their movement can penetrate their opponent's defenses like a bolt of lightning. When the conflict is over, they can return to their naturally calm state and go about their business.

THE KARATE CHOP
If You Could Learn Only One Martial Arts Technique, This Is It!

by Mike Soohey • Photos by Mike Soohey • April 2000

Karate translates as simply "empty hands," but those two words imply that the practitioner can transform his natural physical attributes into formidable weapons without assistance from any mechanical device. One of the most powerful and versatile of those weapons is the knifehand.

The knifehand strike, which the public often calls a "karate chop," is an extremely useful technique that can be employed in a wide assortment of offensive and defensive situations as an attack, block or counterstrike. Because the striking surface—the blade of the hand—is relatively narrow, it is very effective when used against the neck, collarbone, face, ribs, kidneys, groin and joints. Whichever area it attacks, the knifehand is sure to inflict pain.

Foundation

Before learning how the knifehand can be used, it's essential to know how to form the weapon in order to generate maximum power and avoid injury. To make the knifehand, open your hand and hold all four fingers tightly against one another. With your fingers extended, lock your thumb down across your palm and press it firmly backward. Keeping your thumb flexed and held tight against your palm prevents it from being injured during a strike.

Next, keep your little finger straight and stiff as you bend your other three fingers slightly at the first and second joints. The knifehand should be held in this tense state as you make contact with the muscle that runs

The downward knifehand strike targets the opponent's head, neck or shoulders and can be delivered standing or on the ground. (For illustrative purposes, Oleg Taktarov is shown restraining an opponent with a leg lock before delivering a knifehand blow.)

from the base of your little finger to your wrist. To avoid striking with and possibly injuring your little finger, bend your wrist slightly outward and upward. To prevent your fingers from moving and separating, keep them stiff and held tightly together.

The three main variations of the knifehand—inward, outward and downward—usually follow a circular path to the target. When using the technique as a strike or block, it is important to keep your elbow slightly bent so the shock of the impact does not travel directly to your elbow and cause an injury. Executing the technique with a straight arm can also reduce its overall striking force.

Inward Knifehand

The inward knifehand follows a circular motion made in an outward-to-inward arc. If you are striking with your right hand, your initial movement is to raise that hand to the right side of and slightly behind your head. Simultaneously, your left hand moves to the right side of your jaw.

No matter which knifehand or ridgehand variation you choose, you can rest assured that it will serve you well—whether you are engaged in a self-defense drill in the dojo or a street fight in a parking lot.

Power is generated by strongly pulling your left arm across your body as you catapult your striking arm outward.

Offensively, the inward knifehand can be directed at your opponent's face, neck or torso. An ordinary strike can damage a localized area, but a more powerful blow can spread its impact to surrounding tissues, as well. Because the striking surface is small, it can easily reach a target such as the throat or cheek without hitting other obstacles along the way.

In a self-defense situation, the knifehand functions flawlessly. If an assailant grabs your shoulder or arm, he leaves himself open for a vicious inward knifehand to the throat, ribs or spleen. If he rushes at you while telegraphing a rear-hand punch, he can be instantly stopped with an inward chop. If he grabs your lapel, you can deliver a double inward knifehand to the ribs or neck.

As with most hand techniques, stepping forward while executing an

As opponent Brian Thompson (right) tries to grab Mike Soohey, Soohey deflects his arms upward (1). He then chambers his hands (2) and unloads a double knifehand strike to the neck (3).

inward knifehand can produce staggering results. Moving forward not only increases the force and whipping motion behind the blow but also shortens the distance your hand must travel to make contact. The stepping inward knifehand is most often used as a follow-up to a lead-hand parry or block. For example, if an opponent directs a lunge punch at your head, you can parry the strike to one side and follow with an inward knifehand to the face or throat.

Defensively, the inward knifehand can be a forceful blocking technique. It is performed from a fighting stance, side-facing posture or forward-stepping motion. Most often used against a direct attack aimed at your head or upper body, it can create a strong perimeter of defense against the lunge punch, reverse punch, front kick and side kick.

To execute the inward knifehand block, raise your blocking arm slightly behind and beside your head and then swing it forward along a circular path. The blocking action should take place as or just after your forearm crosses in front of your face. To bolster the snapping motion, your other hand should be pulled to the side of your waist as you swing your blocking arm. The point of impact is the blade of your hand. Remember to keep your wrist tight and your elbow slightly bent.

This technique can be used to set up a quick counter for an opponent who attacks along a direct line to your head. When he executes a high lunge punch, you can shove it to the side with a knifehand block and strike with a reverse punch to the body or ridgehand to the neck. Against a front thrust kick, the inward knifehand block enables you to smash the opponent's foot or ankle, stopping the attack and possibly injuring the attacker.

Outward Knifehand

The outward knifehand differs from the inward variation in that your palm faces downward when your hand strikes. Offensively, it can be used to attack the head, neck, shoulders or torso of an assailant. In a life-or-death situation, it can be aimed at the carotid artery or Adam's apple to incapacitate a violent attacker.

To perform the technique, raise your knifehand above your opposite shoulder and turn your palm so it faces the ground or your cheek. Next, swing your hand outward along an arc to the target. Your hand should travel parallel to the floor in a cross-body motion. As it makes contact, be sure your palm faces downward and your digits are tense.

The outward knifehand is perfect for following up after a parry or block. The arm you use to stop the incoming strike can be quickly cocked to the opposite side of your head before you deliver an outward knifehand. To catch your opponent by surprise, this tactic must be performed in one nonstop motion. The key is to deflect his arm or leg from its direct attack line, thus giving you ample room to drive your knifehand into his head or body.

As a blocking technique, the outward knifehand succeeds because of its short arcing motion. It can be used against attacks directed at the middle,

During close-quarters combat, a ridge-hand to the groin can incapacitate an attacker.

Mike Soohey uses a low outward knifehand block to intercept a punch.

upper and lower areas of your body. The short, compact and forceful motion of this technique makes it possible to block most hand and foot strikes. Its circular path makes it effective against arcing strikes such as the roundhouse kick and hook punch.

There are several ways to perform the outward knifehand block; the quickest and most economical is the cross-arm variation, which uses a hard, snapping motion performed from a fighting stance or in conjunction with an advancing or retreating step. It is done by swinging the blocking hand in the same manner as the strike, but you must retract your lead hand and cross the inner section of that forearm on the outer section of your other forearm. As they meet, swing your lead arm in an arc that intercepts the incoming strike and simultaneously withdraw your back hand toward your solar plexus, using it to boost the power of the blocking hand. The palm of that hand will be raised slightly—perhaps pointed at the opponent's legs—because of the twist you impart to your hand just before it makes contact. The blocking action should take place in front of your lead shoulder. Your arm should be bent at 90 degrees to ensure that the blade of your hand makes solid contact with the opponent's weapon.

You can make this block shorter and quicker by not retracting your blocking arm and crossing it over your other arm. This variation can be useful if you face a quick puncher, but it is not as powerful or punishing as the cross-arm method.

The outward knifehand block is a versatile defensive technique that can stop a low attack, as well. Instead of bending your forearm, you simply extend your arm downward and stop just before you lock your elbow. Once again, you should make contact with the blade of your hand.

Even if your outward knifehand block does not halt your opponent's punch or kick, it can easily knock it off-course. That can enable you to move to a superior position and deliver a solid counterattack. If an opponent attempts to drive a roundhouse kick into your gut, you can meet his kicking leg with an outward chop, leaving him wide open for an outward knifehand to the ribs, throat or chin. A lunge or reverse punch aimed at your body or head can be deflected and grabbed by a knifehand block, thus making his body into one big target for your counter.

Downward Knifehand

The downward knifehand is a long, arcing strike that generates tremendous force. It is most often delivered to the shoulders, top of the head and neck. It differs from the inward knifehand in that the striking hand travels vertically rather than horizontally.

To perform the downward knifehand with your right arm, raise your right hand over your right shoulder until it is near your ear. Your elbow should be bent and held slightly higher than when you perform the inward knifehand. This high arm position will allow your hand to accelerate strongly as you swing it downward in a vertical arc. Keep your fingers tight as you snap the blade of your hand into the target. At the moment of contact, pull your other hand toward your waist and twist your hips to harness your body's energy. Remember to keep your elbow slightly bent.

The technique is versatile in that it can be performed on either side of

If martial artists wish to practice the ridgehand strike to the head, proper protection is a must for their partner.

Some hardcore martial artists condition the striking portion of their hands by hitting hard surfaces.

your body. It can also be done from the same ready position that is used in the execution of the inward or outward knifehand. This strategy can be utilized against an opponent who attacks with a jab or lunge punch aimed at your body. As the blow approaches, you parry the punching arm downward and move your defending hand to the opposite shoulder—right where it would be positioned for an outward knifehand. You then surprise your opponent with a downward chop to the collarbone or neck.

When augmented by the momentum of a forward step or jump, the downward knifehand can become a crushing blow. If you block or parry a strike with your lead hand, you can simultaneously cock your rear hand and move your rear knee forward and upward. This high knee position will give the forward step additional momentum to send a powerful downward strike onto the collarbone or head.

The downward knifehand is effective against an adversary who grabs your collar, shoulder or lapel. Once he has ahold of you, you can counter with a straight-line downward chop to the collarbone. As you strike, keep a solid base so you can drive your weapon viciously into the target.

The downward knifehand is primarily an offensive weapon, but it can be used as a strong block in certain situations. If your opponent throws a side or roundhouse kick, you will be able to stop him with a downward block. Because the technique is meant to be delivered with disabling force, you can severely injure the opponent's kicking foot, ankle or entire leg. Because a hand technique generally takes less time to deliver than a foot technique does, a downward knifehand block can easily defeat a kick.

Ridgehand

If you decide to master all the strikes and blocks that can be performed with the knifehand movement, you should not neglect the ridgehand strike. The ridgehand is a knifehand strike in reverse, and it is very effective because of its deceptive path. The strike travels in a wide arc, making it difficult to see as well as to block. Classified as a stunning blow, it can be directed at a wide variety of targets, including the throat, ribs, groin, chin, temple, eyes, nose and carotid arteries. Once you become comfortable performing it, you may find it easier to do than the knifehand.

The three main variations of the knifehand—inward, outward and downward—usually follow a circular path to the target.

The hitting surface of the ridgehand begins at the first knuckle of the index finger and runs to the base of the thumb. The hand is formed in the same manner as the knifehand—with the middle three fingers curled somewhat and the thumb bent under the hand firmly so it stays in contact with the palm at all times. The strike, which starts slightly behind your head or near your hip, follows a horizontal arc similar to that of the inward knifehand.

The ridgehand can be employed after an initial block or parry is made. The act of blocking a head punch or kick can set you up to drive a ridgehand into your opponent's ribs. On the street, the same response could end with a devastating ridgehand to the groin. Or if you have a clear shot to the opponent's face, a ridgehand aimed at his top lip can be quite painful.

No matter which knifehand or ridgehand variation you choose, you can rest assured that it will serve you well—whether you are engaged in a self-defense drill in the *dojo* (training hall) or a street fight in a parking lot.

FANTASTIC HANDS
Jeff Speakman Teaches American *Kenpo's* Trademark Techniques

by Robert W. Young • Photos From Black Belt Archives • November 2000

Since the passing of the legendary Ed Parker in 1990, perhaps no person in American kenpo karate has stood out more than Jeff Speakman. He was personally groomed by Parker to take the art to the masses, and he has succeeded through films such as The Perfect Weapon, Street Knights, The Expert, Deadly Outbreak, Escape From Atlantis, Scorpio One, Land of the Free, Memorial Day and Running Red.

Speakman began his martial arts career in Japanese goju-ryu karate under Lou Angel, a student of Peter Urban. When Speakman graduated from college, Angel told him, "If you want to make the martial arts your life, you should move to California and study kenpo from Ed Parker because he's the best in the world." Speakman immediately packed his bags and waved goodbye to Joplin, Missouri. He didn't stop driving until he hit Pasadena, California, where he spent the next four years mastering the intricacies of the modern fighting art directly under its founder.

Black Belt could think of no one better qualified to explain American kenpo's fantastic hand strikes.

—Editor

People often say that American *kenpo* karate is most renowned for its hand techniques. "If you delve into the art, you will realize that it's a whole-body experience," Jeff Speakman says, "but the thing that stands out most is the hands and their self-defense applications."

"The difference between the way Ed Parker taught and the way other people teach now is the emphasis on the power of the move within the flow of action."
—Jeff Speakman

Kenpo practitioners seldom throw a single hand strike; instead, they prefer to launch a barrage of blows. "It's the philosophy of kenpo to keep a continuation of motion," says Speakman, who was *Black Belt's* 1993

Instructor of the Year. "We call it the concept of continuous flow—of an unbroken flow of energy."

"Opponents of kenpo say we train for 'overkill,' but proponents of kenpo say we train for 'over-skill,' " he continues. "We'd rather teach you too much skill and have you pull it back, as opposed to not having enough skill to save your life."

"My kenpo is a little different from other people's because I emphasize the power and dynamics of the individual strikes I put into a sequence," Speakman says. "Because of what I learned from Lou Angel, who teaches *goju-ryu* karate, I value the Japanese philosophy of the power of the individual strike. I've combined that with the logic and fluidity of kenpo, and the result is dynamic kenpo."

Slap Art?

Kenpo critics frequently label the style a "slap art" because of those rapid-fire hand strikes. Speakman identifies several reasons as the cause.

"In kenpo, there are two categories of striking: minor and major strikes," he says. "But don't be confused because a minor strike can have a major effect. For example, a fingernail whipping across an opponent's eye can be debilitating. Many of the speed strikes in kenpo have that idea behind them."

The problem also stemmed from a dilution of the art that occurred over the years, Speakman says. "Many people hooked onto the speed concept, and that became a selling point. They would think, 'How do I get more students to sign up?' By making them think, 'My God, that guy's so fast! I want to move like him.' But those students were not asking, 'He's fast, but does it also work?'"

"The difference between the way Ed Parker taught and the way other people teach now is the emphasis on the power of the move within the flow of action," Speakman continues. "When I went to his house to train, I felt like I was coming home because that's what I spent all my years in goju-ryu doing—striking with focus, power and intensity. And that's what made him the ultimate practitioner of the art: He had perfect directional harmony, which means that his body and its subtle movements were in perfect direction and harmony with the intention of his strike."

When kenpo is done that way, Speakman says, there is no need to sacrifice power to get speed.

Part of the reputation kenpo has for hand speed stems from what is basically an illusion. "We spend a great deal of time studying the geometry of movement," Speakman says. "For example, instead of making a complete

SELF-DEFENSE AGAINST A LEFT JAB: Jeff Speakman (right) and his opponent square off (1). The opponent punches, and Speakman moves and executes a right inward block with a right vertical punch to the face (2). He follows with a looping downward back-knuckle strike to the ribs, during which his left hand checks the opponent's left arm (3). The *kenpo* stylist then lets loose with a right lifting elbow break (4), a right hammerfist to the bladder (5), a right round kick to the back of the left knee (6), a left round kick to the solar plexus (7) and a right looping punch to the left corner of the jaw (8). Next, Speakman traps the opponent's hand (9) and executes a reverse step-through (10) with a counter-manipulation takedown (11).

193

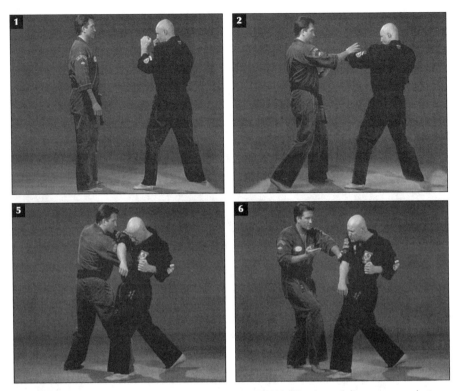

SELF-DEFENSE AGAINST A LEFT-RIGHT PUNCH COMBINATION: Jeff Speakman (left) assumes a ready stance in front of his opponent (1). The opponent throws a left jab, and Speakman counters it with his right arm (2). The opponent then launches a right cross, which Speakman blocks with his left hand (3). The *kenpo* stylist responds with a right inverted fore-knuckle strike to the temple (4) and a right inward collapsing elbow to the ribs (5).

circle with our fist, we make it more of an elliptical move—in other words, we elongate that circle. And by making it a 'shorter' circle, a fist travels through time and space much less, but the impact is just as great as if we made a huge circle."

Additional hand power comes from timing the breath with the movement. "That is organic to my entire martial arts training history," Speakman says. "It is the vehicle that will take you to the release of *chi* (internal energy) within your flow of motion."

Targets

When kenpo students begin training, they often aim their hand strikes at generalized targets. "But as they evolve and better understand the principles and concepts, they learn how to ride the kenpo bike a little better and their

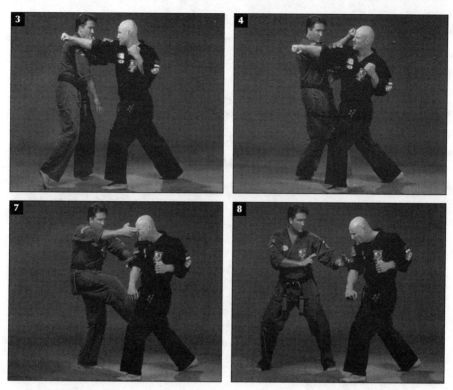

Speakman repositions himself and checks the opponent's right hand downward (6) and executes a right scooping front kick with a simultaneous right-finger eye poke (7). After the barrage, the kenpo stylist settles and observes the damage (8).

targets become more specific," Speakman says. "They manipulate nerves, muscles, tendons and joints; and they use a lot of grappling."

And that's when things really start getting interesting. "We think, 'Striking someone here will make him more open to a successful follow-up strike,'" Speakman says. "A good kenpo practitioner is like a master billiards player: When he opens the rack, he positions all the balls where he wants them, calculates all the angles and runs the table. You don't even have a chance. And that's what it should be like for kenpo practitioners: When they make their move, it's a continuous flow of energy with a premeditated action-reaction-opening-the-next-target-for-my-next-action thought process.

"The phraseology we use is, 'This action creates an angle of opportunity,'" he says. "We predict your most likely reaction to a strike. For example, if we want to punch you in the stomach, we know that your head will come down afterward. So we punch the stomach and maybe our left hand crosses over our right biceps so we can ricochet off the biceps when your head comes down and catch you with a hand sword."

"A good kenpo practitioner is like a master billiards player: When he opens the rack, he positions all the balls where he wants them, calculates all the angles and runs the table."

—Jeff Speakman

Striking a hard target with the delicate bones of the hand can be a risky proposition, Speakman admits: "That's why we form our hand or fist to fit a particular target. If we want to attack the neck, we use an open-hand strike because it has a greater probability of hitting the target without getting injured. Or we might close our hand and use a hammerfist to strike the corner of the jaw because we know we won't be injured by that impact."

Tip of the Iceberg

Perhaps the thing that makes Speakman so devoted to American kenpo is that all the detail and strategy that go into the art's hand strikes can also be found in its kicks and grappling holds. "It's the most inclusive martial art I've ever seen," he says. "It presents such an opportunity for personal and spiritual growth, as well as for self-defense because it covers all potential ranges of a fight."

SLIPPERY AS A SNAKE
The Elusive Lead of Bruce Lee's *Jeet Kune Do*

by William Holland • Photos by Andrea Starick • January 2001

Bruce Lee belongs to that select group of martial artists who accomplished so much during their life that they changed the way the world fought. Although part of his success stemmed from his phenomenal physique and rapid reflexes, much of it was because of the highly effective tools and techniques he chose to focus on. One of them was the "elusive lead."

Strong-Side Lead

Lee bucked convention when he insisted that your strong arm be put in the lead (or forward) position. Although that may seem unconventional to boxers and traditional martial artists, weapons systems such as fencing and *kali* apply the strong-side-lead concept quite successfully.

What are the advantages of the strong-side lead? For one, it puts your strongest weapon closer to your opponent, enabling it to be used more frequently. Because it is your dominant hand, it is probably more accurate, quick, powerful and coordinated; and because it is your strong side, you can generate more natural power without having to use as much body movement. Thus, your jab and lead hooks can be deployed with quick and devastating results while you maintain economy and simplicity of motion.

Not only does the elusiveness of the strike make it difficult for him to time and predict your entry, but the technique also incorporates a varying of the defensive positions of your head and limbs.

That Lee held the lead punch in the highest regard is evidenced by a passage from his *Tao of Jeet Kune Do:* "The leading straight punch is the backbone of all punching in *jeet kune do*. It is used as an offensive and defensive weapon to stop and intercept an opponent's complex attack at a moment's notice. The leading straight punch is the fastest of all punches. With minimum movements involved in delivery, balance is not disturbed, and because it goes straight toward the target, it has a better chance of landing."

Longest Weapon, Nearest Target

When attacking or intercepting, the JKD fighter uses predominantly

Jeet kune do instructor Bill Holland (right) sizes up his prey (1) and then draws him out of his defensive position with a low, probing feint (2). Before the opponent can recover, Holland scores with a progressive indirect back-hand punch (3).

punches to the upper body and head while keeping kicks confined to the midsection and below. When attacking, he often strikes with his lead hand or foot while parrying with his rear hand. That maintains the economy and directness of the lead punch by not entangling those lead tools for defensive purposes. This fighting principle is called using the longest weapon to attack the nearest target.

In JKD, defense is often employed with shifting and evasive footwork and body movement, slipping and bobbing rather than blocking or making contact with the opponent's weapon. When contact is made, it is often done with a light parrying motion with the rear hand. That keeps the lead hand out of the line of engagement and free to hit the unsuspecting opponent.

Serpent's Tongue

In addition to maintaining a constantly shifting body and head, Lee advocated keeping the lead hand in a state of motion. Darting in and out like the tongue of a snake, your lead hand can be used with quick, broken rhythm to upset the opponent's timing, confusing him or inducing him briefly into a trancelike state.

This movement also provides momentum before a lead punch or strike—somewhat like having a running start at the beginning of a race. Known as the "hammer principle," this moving start works like a stone skipping off a lake, with the punch picking up speed and rotation as it ricochets off an imaginary wall.

The movement of the serpent's tongue should be crisp and economical, moving in and out, up and down, worrying and bothering the eyes and timing of the adversary. As he watches the quick movements of your lead hand, that hand can be used to fake or open avenues for your rear hand and other weapons.

Felt Before It Is Seen

By constantly moving your lead hand, you have the advantage of what Lee called "choice reaction." In other words, by watching not only your flicking lead hand but also your shifting body, the opponent must analyze and choose how to respond to various potentially dangerous stimuli, thereby slowing his reaction time.

Unlike many classical styles of fighting, JKD emphasizes not having a set posture or stance. With your lead hand constantly moving and your feet and body shifting continually, you must be able to strike at any time from wherever your hand happens to be. The strike should be executed without your having to assume a certain position for power. You should practice striking with your lead hand in motion, from various positions or gates, and immediately after a fake or parry without chambering it.

Lead vs. Counterpunchers

The elusive lead is a superb tactic to employ against a counterpuncher. Not only does the elusiveness of the strike make it difficult for him to time and predict your entry, but the technique also incorporates a varying of the defensive positions of your head and limbs.

While changing the position of your lead hand before the delivery of a strike, you should also vary the position of your head, rear hand, body and returning hand when you attack. That will upset his intentions.

For extra precaution against that type of fighter, you can also change the position of your rear guarding hand as well as the position to which you return your lead hand. If you do so, he will have no clue as to where your head will be—nor will he have a fix on your rear- or lead-hand guard positions. That will further interrupt his game plan.

Angular Attacks

In JKD, much weight is given to striking directly and efficiently in a straight line because it is the shortest distance between two points. However, a skilled opponent will know this, too, and will strive to take the direct line away. Thus, the elusive lead is used to strike along a straight line when it is available and along a curved line when it is necessary.

Depending on the defensive positions of the opponent's guard, you may at one moment use a straight blast to the centerline and at another moment use a backfist, corkscrew hook or low-line jab to avoid his defensive tools and strike his most vulnerable target.

With your lead hand constantly moving, you should be able to deploy these various strikes from assorted positions of transition. For instance, if the opponent is standing in a left lead and leaves his left temple exposed, you can deliver, from a right lead, a right corkscrew jab from a low position, high position, centerline position, outer-gate position, and inner- or outer-perimeter position—all while moving.

Progressive Indirect Attacks

Another primary tactic of JKD is the progressive indirect attack. It uses your lead hand or foot to initiate the attack, and when the opponent moves his guard to defend, your lead hand continues at a divergent angle

---

In addition to maintaining a constantly shifting body and head, Lee advocated keeping the lead hand in a state of motion.

---

to strike the newly exposed target.

Whereas many fighters fake with one weapon and score with a different one, the progressive indirect attack utilizes the same weapon to create the opening and then immediately strike it. That is particularly advantageous as your lead weapon is already halfway to the target.

With the power and economic explosiveness learned from the one- and three-inch floating punch, you can unload a tremendous amount of torque and penetration with a minimal amount of movement or muscular effort. So while the progressive indirect attack travels a relatively short distance from the transition point of the feint, your entire body unloads with whip-like speed to inflict a lot of pain and damage.

In all strikes, your weapon should be deployed before the rest of your body, thereby saving the maximum amount of rotation and power for the moment of impact. The movement of your hips, torso, legs and shoulders is unleashed just as your weapon makes contact; it allows the payload of power from your body to be dumped on the opponent's body and not wasted en route.

As Lee wrote in *Tao of Jeet Kune Do,* "You never strike your opponent with your fist only; you strike him with your whole body." To try to muscle up and hit with a lot of muscular force from your arm is like trying to throw a nail into a board. It is more efficient to place the nail (your fist) onto the target and apply force with the hammer (your legs, hips and torso).

Doubling Up

A "redoublement" is two rapid consecutive blows to the same target with the same weapon. It can be very fruitful against a fighter who merely leans away or slips his head slightly to avoid your first jab or strike. He leaves his guard down or out of the line of attack because he believes that a simple evasive move will be sufficient. Because his defensive guard is not

Knowing his opponent has a quick lead-hand block, Bill Holland (right) sets him up to engage his front-line defense (1). Holland's lead-hand strike is blocked (2), but the opponent drops his blocking hand after its mission is accomplished (3). Holland then snaps out a penetrating "redoublement" backfist (4).

Against an opponent who diligently protects his head, Bill Holland (right) uses an elusive lead that attacks the most vulnerable target: the midsection.

obstructing your line of attack, another strike on the same line coupled with an advancing step can drive your second blow through the target. Often, a fighter who leans or slips away immediately will return his head to its original position, thereby increasing the impact of your second strike.

Another type of fighter who lends himself to being hit with the redoublement is the one who quickly parries your first blow but takes his parrying hand back away from the attack line, thereby exposing the line for your follow-up hit. You can penetrate the small crevice he creates by pulling his parrying hand away with the redoublement because his attacking hand does not return all the way back to its original position, striking instead from half to three-quarters of a recoil.

Ricochet Hit

When confronted by a skilled defender who does not open himself up to the redoublement, you can try another proven elusive-lead tactic: the "ricochet hit." It is similar to the redoublement in that it uses lead-hand strikes in rapid succession. The difference is that you use a different angle, level or target with the second blow. Examples include a lead jab-lead hook combination, a low jab-high backfist combination and a lead backfist-lead ridgehand combination.

The ricochet hit is similar to the progressive indirect attack in that the same weapon is used twice; however, the first movement must be meant to score and not merely to act as a feint. As Lee was fond of saying: When in doubt, hit.

As the defender gets hit by, parries, blocks or evades your initial backfist, he may inadvertently expose the other side of his head to a ridgehand or hook. If you drive a penetrating low jab into his ribs, his reaction to getting hit or his attempt to keep from getting hit may cause him to lower his guard and expose himself to a quick backfist. The key to making the ricochet hit succeed is ensuring that the initial strike places your lead hand in close proximity to him, thereby reducing the distance and travel time.

Cutting Edge

The elusive lead can take your fighting skill to a higher level. When using it, keep the following principles in mind:

- Remain loose and relaxed with crisp, shifting movements.
- Make each strike brief and explosive between longer periods of relaxation.
- Be predictably unpredictable.
- Use movement and body torque, not the swinging force of your arm, to supply the power.
- Let your hand be the nail and your body be the hammer.
- Hit like a bullwhip, not like a ball and chain.
- Be able to strike at any time, at any target, from any position and at any angle.

ISSHIN-RYU PLUS
Karate Legend Gary Alexander Updates an Old Art for a New Millennium
by Floyd Burk • Photos From the Black Belt Archives • April 2001

Isshin-ryu karate legend and *Black Belt* Hall of Fame member Gary Alexander has always been a get-on-the-mat-and-see-what-you-can-do kind of guy. Rugged and tough, this decorated Marine Corps veteran is the John Wayne of the martial arts world. In the late 1950s, he began making a name for himself by beating the top karate stylists in bare-knuckle sparring matches. By taking on all comers, he helped his art become a respected form of unarmed combat; and by beating them to a pulp, he earned a reputation as the "hammer of isshin-ryu."

These days, the Edison, New Jersey-based Alexander is busier than ever teaching a modified version of isshin-ryu, which he simply refers to as "isshin-ryu plus." It is a hybrid system that just makes good sense: a solid foundation of original isshin-ryu on which stands a unique blend of Alexander's own techniques and principles. Those improvements make the system fit the practitioner rather than forcing the practitioner to fit the system, he claims. The following are some of the major modernizations.

Potent Punch

Isshin-ryu plus teaches two essentials for maximizing the effectiveness of your punches: in-line chambering and pistonlike delivery and recoil. To derive the greatest benefit from these improvements, you must bring your fist as far back and as high as you can—near the upper part of your rib cage—and you must align your elbow directly behind it. When you launch the punch, send it out and yank it back in the same way a piston moves inside a cylinder. Do not pause between the delivery and the retraction.

This isshin-ryu plus method differs from the more popular punching techniques that involve beginning the blow with your fist positioned near your face or hip. It is also different from those that allow you to hold your elbow low and out of alignment with your fist. Executing the strike with a misaligned elbow can lead to a loss of power and control because the punch will often skip off the target the same way the tip of a pool stick skips off the cue ball when the shooter has misaligned it.

The combination of in-line chambering and piston action allows you to attain pinpoint accuracy and maximum shock and penetration with your punch. You can fire the same technique over and over like a jackhammer while you maneuver for the best position, Alexander says.

Better Backfist

"When it comes to performing the backfist, a lot of people make the mistake of throwing it and executing the follow-through with their entire arm extended," Alexander says. "This will not only get your arm broken, but it will also make it easy for your adversary to block the technique. I've had my own arm broken at the elbow while doing the backfist the old-fashioned way—that's why I changed it."

PLUS PUNCH: Gary Alexander (right) faces opponent Bill Miller in a fighting stance (1). Alexander grabs Miller's lead arm and chambers his left fist high on his rib cage (2). The *isshin-ryu* plus master then drives his fist straight out (3) and pulls it straight back (not shown) like a piston in a cylinder.

PLUS BACKFIST: Gary Alexander (right) faces Bill Miller (1). Alexander cocks his right fist near his left shoulder (2) and lets it fly with the strike (3).

To perform the backfist the isshin-ryu plus way, first aim the elbow of your striking arm at the target and move that fist to the opposite side of your head. Next, using a circular motion with your elbow at the center, unleash the technique and let your fist travel until it makes an impact and then retract it like a whip. Remember to move only your forearm. Although the backfist travels along an arc, the quick retraction will ensure that it is safe as well as effective.

To conceptualize how the whipping action can turn a ho-hum technique designed for tournaments into a devastating heavy hitter for the street, Alexander says, think about snapping someone with a towel. It's not the outward motion that plants a welt on the receiving end; rather, it's the snap that takes place once the tip of the towel reaches maximum extension.

Gnarly Knifehand

The knifehand Alexander incorporated into isshin-ryu plus is the vertical (or slightly angled) version of the strike. To understand its mechanics, begin by swinging your open right hand up to the right side of your head. Then let the knifehand fly into the target using an arcing trajectory and the same pistonlike delivery and retraction.

The related hammerfist strike of isshin-ryu plus is performed in the

The whipping action at the termination of the blow is the key to its effectiveness (4).

same manner, except with your hand closed. "In the old-fashioned method, centrifugal force is not emphasized and the techniques are much shorter and choppier," Alexander says. "That renders the strikes less effective than the way we do them."

Effective Elbow

The isshin-ryu plus elbow strike also employs centrifugal force and pistonlike action, and the impact is made with the tip of the bone for maximum penetration.

To execute it, chamber the weapon by positioning your right fist near your right shoulder and leaving your elbow pointed downward. (Think of holding an ice-cream cone in your hand and jamming it, ice cream first, into your shoulder.) Your limb does not pause in this position; rather, the elbow immediately blasts upward or horizontally and is retracted. That keeps you from exposing yourself to a counterattack executed the moment you lock out the strike.

Combat Kicks

"In standard isshin-ryu and isshin-ryu plus, the kicks all chamber up and piston out and back," Alexander says. "But when you kick, you've got to be able to sneak your foot into the target. The average fighter's radar zone is about 45 degrees up, down and to the side. Since most kicks come at him inside his radar zone, he can easily block or grab your leg and take you to the ground."

"So you have to build a better mousetrap," Alexander continues. "Isshin-ryu plus uses different angles of attack—ones that most people don't see or use—and it teaches you to whip the kicks in at angles your opponent does not expect them to come from."

When doing the front snap kick and roundhouse kick, Alexander says, you should raise your knee high enough to use it as a kind of sighting device. That action should culminate with your calf muscle "bouncing off" your hamstring muscle, after which you let the kick fly. Do not attempt to kick to a level that is higher than the level at which you can point and hold your knee, he advises.

When doing the isshin-ryu plus back kick, raise your knee and keep your lower leg parallel to the ground. Cock your foot high, hold it tight against your buttocks and then blast the kick out and back like a piston, Alexander says.

Corrected Kata

Naturally, isshin-ryu plus has a different take on *kata* (forms). "Many

PLUS KNIFEHAND: Gary Alexander (right) confronts his opponent (1). Alexander raises his lead arm and his striking arm (2)

martial artists, especially those with little or no real combat time, practice their kata in a way that is diametrically opposed to the way they fight," Alexander says. "This amounts to a loss of precious training time."

"That's why isshin-ryu plus uses the 10 kata of standard isshin-ryu with slight modifications to the choreography," Alexander continues. "An example of one of those modifications is when a traditional movement puts the practitioner down on his knee; we stay up and just take a wider, lower-profile stance to maintain mobility."

Alexander's formulas for improved striking have also been incorporated into the kata of isshin-ryu plus. "By doing them the same way we fight, our movements stay fluid and relaxed," he says. "Our kata have a lot of fight in them, and they are done with the objective of enhancing the student's maneuverability and striking skills, and for learning effective strategies."

Inescapable Conclusion

After prevailing in numerous fistfights and a myriad of sparring matches, Alexander created isshin-ryu plus as a combat-effective hybrid art for the 20th century. Drawing from his 40-plus years of training men, women and children from all walks of life—including numerous police officers and military personnel—he then honed it into the finely tuned system it is today. As the world eases into the 21st century, Alexander remains confident that

and then uses his left hand to trap his opponent's lead hand (3) before slamming his knifehand into the back of his neck (4). Afterward, Alexander immediately retracts the striking limb.

his art will continue to meet the needs of martial artists around the world who prefer to stay on the cutting edge of self-defense without abandoning their traditional karate roots.

5 Combat Tips From the Master

- **Defense is offense:** Seek to inflict damage on your opponent with your blocking techniques and use them to create openings so you can launch effective counterattacks.
- **Never underestimate your opponent:** Do not take your opponent too lightly; it could get you hurt or killed. Fight every opponent as if he were a highly trained master.
- **Don't stop at one:** When you attack, use a sequence of at least five hits. The bad guy may block the first or second shot, but sooner or later, one will get in.
- **Use typhooning:** If you must fight multiple attackers or find yourself in a situation in which things get crazy, "typhooning" can save your life: Keep your hands and feet moving, shift your body, execute sweeps and trips, try to throw your opponent, and blast away with as many strikes as possible. The key is to overwhelm him.
- **Be true to your training:** You must believe in what you are doing. No workout should be done in a sloppy fashion or like a weekend hobby. Stay true to your art by training as if your life depended on it.

—F.B.

MODIFIED HAND STRIKES

by Jim Wagner • May 2001

I am 5 feet 10 inches tall, weigh 190 pounds and have extensive hand-to-hand training and experience. Now, let me give you two scenarios, and afterward you will see how they relate to you.

Scenario one: For reasons unknown, a 6-foot-3-inch, 230-pound man walks over and tries to strike me with his closed fist. I block it and then throw a solid jab-cross combination into his face, inadvertently breaking his nose in the process. Was my action justified? Is this a legitimate self-defense situation?

Scenario two: A woman who stands 5 feet tall and tips the scales at 110 pounds approaches me. For no reason, she takes a swing at me with her closed fist. To defend myself, I throw the same jab-cross combination and bust her nose. Is this also a legitimate self-defense situation?

In both scenarios, my actions were indeed justified. No matter what part of the country you live in, the penal code gives you the authority to defend yourself against bodily injury or the immediate threat thereof. In the scenarios described above, the man and the woman both tried to harm me, so I had the right to protect myself. Nobody would argue this point.

However, regardless of my right to defend myself, I run the risk of being accused of using excessive force on the woman. It's not merely a gender issue, either. If I strike a person who is weaker or less skilled than I am, that person will probably use these facts against me in a criminal and civil lawsuit.

When the police arrive or I stand before a jury, they are likely to conclude that my actions to defend myself against the larger man were justified. However, no jury in the world will say I was justified in breaking the smaller woman's nose with the technique I used. Although I may be acquitted of the criminal charges, I will most likely face a civil suit for using excessive force. Such horror stories don't just happen to cops but also to well-meaning citizens trying to defend themselves.

The problem with most martial arts training today is what I call the "generic-attacker syndrome," and it is yet another area in which civilian training lags behind military and law-enforcement training. Although you may picture the military as always destroying buildings and killing people, many of today's operations are actually peacekeeping missions. They must undergo nonlethal training (crowd control, riot situations, prisoner handling, etc.) if they are going on foreign deployments. In law enforcement, peace officers must adhere to the use-of-force continuum, in which only reasonable force can be used in any particular situation.

From my own martial arts background and what I observe when I visit schools around the world, most self-defense techniques seem geared toward worst-case scenarios, not for encounters with weaker subjects. Now that I look back, most of my fights as a street cop have been with inferior opponents who wanted to take me on. Only a handful of altercations have been serious ones in which the combatants were trying to do me harm.

When I teach combatives courses to law-enforcement and military personnel, I always cover fist strikes. Although most people would refer to it as "punching," I teach students not to use that word because it has

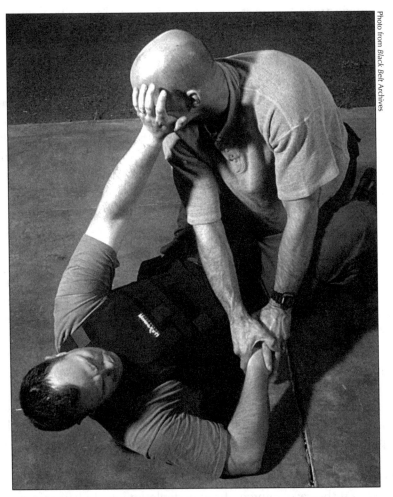

Photo from Black Belt Archives

In combatives courses, Jim Wagner (bottom) teaches "modified open-hand Olympic boxing techniques" for use against weaker assailants.

negative connotations. To most people, "punch" sounds hard and solid, while "hit with a closed fist" sounds more civilized. For this reason, police in the United States avoid using any martial arts terminology.

But even if you use this milder wording in defense of your striking a weaker subject, it still isn't going to fly. You need more than just a change of words; you need to modify your techniques.

Therefore, when striking is called for against a weaker subject, I teach students to hit with "modified open-hand Olympic boxing techniques." You can still strike the subject with the traditional jab, cross and hook, but your hand will be open. For example, instead of striking with your knuckles, you strike with your palm. The moment your palm makes contact with the target, you pull it in instantly rather than drive it through. More specifically, to throw a modified open-hand Olympic boxing jab, you don't drive your palm through to the back of the other guy's head; you rake your palm downward at the moment of impact. When throwing a modified open-hand Olympic boxing hook, you suddenly whip your hand toward your own body instead of following through on the trajectory, "pulling the punch" slightly. It's basically slapping.

With this politically correct mind-set, let's take the second scenario and add the "spin" to it.

I'm sitting in court, and the defense attorney points to his female client, who is wearing a neck brace and a bandage on her nose, and says, "You punched my client right in the face and broke her nose, didn't you, Sergeant Wagner?" I answer, "No, I didn't." Of course, the defense attorney calls me a liar, so I explain: "That woman swung at my face with a closed fist. To defend myself against injury, I reacted by using a modified open-hand Olympic boxing jab and cross combination to stop her. In other words, I simply slapped her. I could have used a closed fist, but I wanted to avoid injuring her."

The main point of this illustration is that I used my training in my favor by articulating that I purposefully used less force than I could have. To the jury and the police, it sounds a lot better than having responded in generic-defense mode because telling them that I did what I did because I was trained that way is not a valid defense.

To better prepare yourself for real self-defense, don't fall into the generic-attacker syndrome. When you spar, imagine you are going up against a weaker opponent and adjust your techniques accordingly. By training for these situations now, you will condition yourself to use a lower level of force when you fight, thus reducing your liability.

10 LAWS OF THE FIST
Kenpo's Principles for Certain Victory in Combat
by Charles Mattera • Photos by Sara Fogan • April 2002

For decades, *kenpo* has been renowned in the West as one of the most effective and efficient martial arts in existence, and for hundreds of years before that it enjoyed a similar reputation in Asia. Much of that success can be attributed to a set of fighting principles that has been defined and refined into an exact science through the efforts of scores of masters who knew the meaning of trial by fire. This article will outline 10 of those laws for the benefit of all the martial artists who have not had the opportunity to experience them firsthand.

Law of the Circle and the Line

The first law of kenpo states that, when your opponent charges straight in and attacks, you should use your feet to move your body along a circular path. You should also consider moving your arms in a circular pattern to deflect the oncoming force.

When your opponent attacks you in a circular fashion, however, you should respond with a fast linear attack—along a straight line from your weapon to his target. Just as the circle can overcome the line, the line can overcome the circle.

Law of 'Strike First'

This principle has several meanings. First, it indicates that kenpo is primarily a striking art. Seventy percent hands and 30 percent feet is the classical breakdown, but you can change the proportion according to the circumstances or your body build.

The second meaning is that, if a confrontation is inevitable—a thug is climbing through your bathroom window at 2 o'clock in the morning and he starts swinging a baseball bat—you should not wait for the aggressor to attack first. You need to hit him first with a foot, a fist, an elbow or a knee. You also need to hit hard and hit continuously until he is subdued.

The kenpo curriculum also includes numerous grappling and throwing techniques, but research has shown they are used in less than 25 percent of the encounters practitioners have found themselves in and they are ineffective against multiple attackers. Because grappling uses four times as much strength and energy as striking does, it has been deemed a last resort suitable for use only if your opponent penetrates your first and second lines of defense: your feet and fists, respectively.

Law of Multiple Strikes

Kenpo is different from many karate styles in that it teaches you to strike first and strike often in rapid succession—high, low, straight in and along a circular path. While unleashing such rapid-fire strikes, it becomes difficult to *kiai* (shout) in conjunction with each one. Therefore, you should forget about issuing a kiai with each blow; in fact, doing so means you are expending excess energy.

Your first and second strikes should be designed to stun, distract and slow your opponent. Your third and, if necessary, fourth strikes are the power blows. Remember the kenpo maxim: First set your opponent up and then take him out.

Law of Targets

If you had to punch a hole through a wall, would you rather hit a half-inch of sheetrock or a 2-by-4 stud? The answer is obvious, and it's also why kenpo

LAW OF THE CIRCLE AND THE LINE: As Jack Turner (right) executes a linear front kick, Charles Mattera steps forward and stops it with a cross-hand block (1). Mattera then redirects the foot with a circular parry, throwing the opponent off-balance (2). Next, he darts in and effects a right ridgehand *shuto* strike to the other man's throat (3).

LAW OF MULTIPLE STRIKES: The opponent (right) punches, and Charles Mattera moves to the outside, using his left hand to check-block and his right to execute a circular backfist (1). He then drops into a horse stance and delivers a left elbow to the opponent's floating ribs (2), followed by a right palm heel to

advocates striking "soft" targets. No one ever broke his knuckle punching an attacker's temple, no one ever fractured his instep kicking an attacker's groin and no one ever injured his knifehand striking an attacker's throat.

In Japan, the *makiwara* board is used to toughen the hands, and in Thailand, *muay Thai* fighters harden their shins by kicking banana trees. Kenpo is different in that it teaches the path of least resistance and least pain. Precisely targeting the temple, face, nose, neck, solar plexus, stomach, groin and floating ribs is superior to simply pummeling away on random parts of the aggressor's body.

Law of Kicking

Kenpo's mandate to kick low is based on logic. A roundhouse kick and spinning reverse crescent kick to the head may be flashy and impressive, but such maneuvers take longer to execute because your leg has to travel farther. They also expose your groin to your opponent's kick.

Because kicking high requires superior balance and focus, you should practice your leg techniques high but deliver them low for self-defense. Furthermore, kicking low to the legs—executing a "pillar attack" in kenpo-speak—can break your opponent's balance and his leg.

the jaw (3) and a left ridgehand to the other side of the jaw (4). To finish, Mattera steps backward while using his left arm to choke and his right hand to claw the eyes (5).

Law of 'No Block'

Kenpo emphasizes economy of movement and economy of time. Hence, its no-block principle teaches that to avoid being struck by a punch or kick, you should move your body out of harm's way. The most advanced defense taught in the martial arts, it was perhaps best expressed by the old Shaolin priest in the *Kung Fu* television series: "Avoid rather than check; check rather than block; block rather than strike; strike rather than hurt; hurt rather than maim; maim rather than kill—for all life is precious."

Strategically, a block is a wasted move because it does not stop your opponent from attacking again with his free limb. It is much better to move yourself out of the way of his punch or kick and simultaneously counterattack. This way of fighting is reserved for brown belts and above, however, because it requires a higher level of skill to employ correctly and a significant amount of sparring experience to avoid the tendency to allow your feet to stick to the ground during the crisis your brain senses.

The no-block principle does not mean blocking plays no part in fighting.

LAW OF KICKING AND LAW OF THE CIRCLE AND THE LINE: Charles Mattera is seized by two attackers (1). He immediately steps backward and raises his arms overhead along a circular path to lock the opponents' arms and throw them off-balance (2-3). The *kenpo* expert then smashes a side blade kick into the back of one man's knee (4) and a low roundhouse into the back of the other man's knee (5-6). Mattera finishes with a double bear-paw strike to the ears (7).

If you were standing in a corner with no way out and an assailant charged with a club, you would have to block his attack. That's why kenpo teaches eight distinct blocking systems, along with dozens of traps, yet they all lead to the same maxim: The best block of all is no block at all.

Law of Yielding and Redirecting

Yielding and redirecting are best exemplified by the symbol of *yin* and *yang* (soft and hard). When your opponent attacks hard, you should counterattack soft. If he is weaker than you or attacks soft, you should counterattack hard to end the encounter quickly and directly.

Aikido includes many techniques that rely on the same principle of yielding and redirecting. In most karate systems, however, blocking is extremely hard and may injure not only the attacker but also the blocker. For the most part, kenpo does not adhere to this concept of "a block is a strike." Instead, it teaches you to block soft and strike hard.

Redirecting is also of paramount importance. Many arts teach their practitioners to use a downward block to stop a front kick, resulting in the student's hammerfist being slammed into the attacker's instep, but such an impact can break the blocking hand or arm. Kenpo teaches that it is preferable to parry your opponent's leg to the side and spin him off-balance before you counterattack hard. Such a redirecting movement will usually disrupt his balance and leave him vulnerable.

Law of Mobility

Mobility may be the easiest kenpo principle to understand. It holds that a moving target is harder to hit than a stationary one. As basic as that sounds, many martial artists fail to implement it.

Kenpo teaches that there are three types of fighters: the statue, who has little mobility and will not retreat; the runner, who has to be chased around the ring; and the steamroller, who just keeps coming at you. If you are any one of these, be careful because you are predictable and can thus be defeated. To transcend mediocrity, you must mix things up, and no matter what, keep moving. If your stance is upright and your movement is good, you will be able to put yourself in a superior position relative to your opponent.

Law of Flexibility

The law of flexibility is the law of survival. Kenpo is unique in that it adapts to your build, personality and spirit. If you stand 4 feet 10 inches tall, it makes little sense for you to focus on kicking when your greatest strengths may be mobility and quickness. If you are a 110-pound woman, it makes little sense for you to grapple with a 230-pound assailant. The old kenpo masters showed their wisdom when they proclaimed that, in a fight for your life, you should use what you know best and forget about the sanctity of the style.

Every practitioner has different attributes that can make him or her effective. A tall person with long legs may have an advantage with kicking, a short person may have an advantage with his hands and a heavy person may have an advantage in grappling. The law of flexibility allows them all to develop their own repertoire of techniques from within kenpo.

Law of the Warrior Spirit

The final principle of kenpo is composed of two essential components: the internal and external. A rabid dog may pose a formidable threat, but it possesses only the external component of the warrior spirit. Inside, the animal is not thinking. To have a complete warrior spirit, you must be ferocious on the outside but calm and tranquil on the inside.

Samurai warriors used to say that any day is a good day to die. That did not mean they sought death. On the contrary, they wanted to preserve life—especially their own. But they knew that, if they went into battle with fear in their heart, they could die or sustain a serious injury. They knew that only by embracing and accepting death could they focus everything on the physical task at hand: defeating the enemy.

Your kiai, facial expressions, stance and on-guard position must all work in unison. Following the principle of yin and yang, you should be hard on the outside and soft on the inside. When used in this way, warrior spirit can be more important than physical skill.

Key to Success

Perhaps the best way to put the 10 laws of kenpo into practice is to think of them as keys that can unlock the doors of higher learning. Remember that they are not written in stone, because there are exceptions to every rule.

In the 35 years I have practiced kenpo, I have discovered only one negative side to the 10 laws: A single lifetime is not enough to learn everything there is to know about them. No doubt many martial artists would consider that a positive.

Maximum Mobility

One of the best mobility-enhancing exercises you can do is list all the basic stances your art teaches: cat stance, front stance, bow-and-arrow stance, leaning stance, kneeling stance, twist stance, crane stance and so on. Then regularly devote a workout session to combining all those stances with all the possible ways your art teaches you to move from one to another. You'll be amazed at all the mobility possibilities that will soon become second nature. Remember that fighting is like a chess game in that the more options you afford yourself, the better off you are.

— C.M.

SPIN DOCTOR
Shonie Carter Teaches Three Variations of the Technique That Made Him Famous!

by S.D. Seong • Photos by Robert W. Young • August 2002

Shonie Carter insists that his fame in the martial arts world does not stem from his ability to score with any particular technique, but from his ability to use his unorthodox fighting strategy to triumph over opponents who are considered virtual shoo-ins. Nevertheless, fans of the mixed martial arts remember him best for the spinning techniques he used against Matt Serra in the Ultimate Fighting Championship 31.

"I like to surprise my opponents by doing something I haven't been working on, something they don't expect," Carter says. "When I fought Matt in the UFC, I hadn't been working on the spinning backfist. The biggest assets I have are versatility and a willingness to execute a technique that most people wouldn't think of doing."

For the sake of *Black Belt* readers who wish to boost their versatility and take their opponent by surprise with a spinning attack, Carter agreed to reveal the secrets of three variations of his most feared technique.

Spinning Forearm

Carter's favorite implementation of the spinning forearm begins with a left jab that is not really supposed to make contact with the opponent's jaw. Its main function is to elicit a response such as a lead-leg front kick. Once that foot is launched, Carter says, you block it with your lead hand and push it to your left (to the opponent's inside). At the same time, step to the outside of his lead leg, which prevents him from having a clean shot at your jaw.

"As you torque your hip, you have to protect your chin by burying it into your left shoulder; otherwise, he will be able to hit you with a straight right," he says. "Don't extend your arm until you spin and look over your right shoulder to see where your target is because he may have moved into you. As soon as you see him, you can gauge whether you should throw the forearm or a variation of the spinning technique."

Distance is the factor that determines whether the spinning forearm, spinning elbow or spinning backfist should be used, Carter says: "When your target is his head, you really want to make full contact with it. You don't want the impact to be diffused, which happens when you are falling away from him. You want him to be moving into it, and you want to see that he's dropped his hands enough for you to land your forearm right across his mandible."

Spinning Backfist

Carter's spinning backfist begins with you and your opponent standing just outside of punching range. You set him up by launching a left jab and then a right cross. His reaction is minimal because of the limited nature of the threat. You then step to the outside of his lead leg as you execute a left cross that intentionally misses. Having just moved in close, you are in perfect position to begin to spin.

"Once you close the distance by stepping in, you create the torque within your hip to maximize the impact force," Carter says. "Because an object

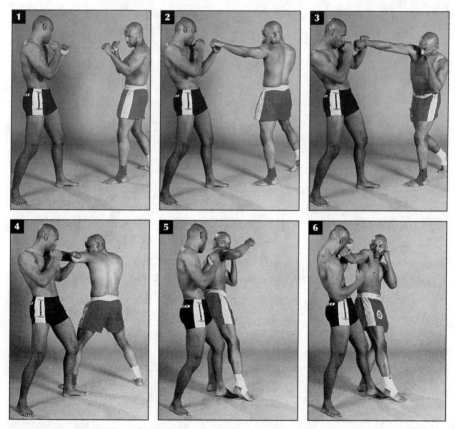

SPINNING BACKFIST: The opponent (left) faces Shonie Carter (1). Carter sets him up with a left jab (2) and a right cross (3), then uses a jab and a step to position his left foot outside the opponent's left foot (4). Next, Carter begins spinning clockwise and locks his eyes on the opponent's head as soon as possible (5). He finishes by extending his arm and making contact with his fist (6).

at the end of a lever moves faster than an object at the center, the energy from your hip is transferred to your backfist, which moves very fast. It hits his jaw and sends it back into his skull, jarring his brain. If you want to go high, your fist can catch him in the temple region."

It is essential to maintain proper balance during the execution of this technique, Carter says, so you can recover quickly should you miss the target. Staying balanced will also help you if your opponent gets to your back while you are momentarily facing away from him. "If that happens, don't freak out," he says. "Spin like a top to create centrifugal force; and as you twist and he tries to clinch, throw techniques. You'll be so sweaty that you'll probably get out of his hold and end up right in front of him."

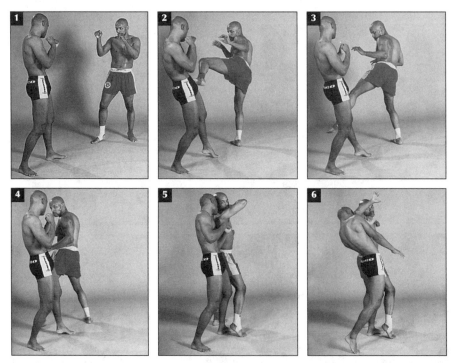

SPINNING ELBOW: Shonie Carter (right) and his opponent square off outside of kicking range (1). Carter executes a rear-leg roundhouse kick (2) and sets his foot down to the outside of the opponent's lead foot (3). While watching the other man (4), Carter starts his clockwise spin (5). To avoid the opponent's defenses, he swings his elbow downward at a 45-degree angle, striking the cheek (6).

Spinning Elbow

The third version of Carter's spinning methodology relies on the elbow for the impact. You and your opponent start just outside of kicking range. Pivot on your lead foot as you deliver a rear-leg roundhouse kick. As your foot passes its target, plant it on the floor to the outside of his lead foot. That movement puts you close enough to initiate your spin.

"As you protect your chin and turn, you must look over your shoulder to track the target," Carter says. "To avoid his defense, you want to come over the top of his hands and drop your elbow on him at a 45-degree angle right across the temple, the eye, the bridge of the nose and the cheek. Somewhere in there, something will bleed. It might not knock him out, but it will give him a black eye, a broken nose or a cut cheek bone."

The spinning elbow can also be used for self-defense, Carter says: "When I was a bouncer, I had to use elbows all the time. They're especially good when you don't have room to kick. A short-range elbow hitting a bony surface tends to get someone's attention fast."

Spin Training

Carter advises caution whenever you work on your spinning forearm, spinning backfist or spinning elbow in the *dojo*. "It's hard to slow them down, especially if you're not that experienced," he says. "Always have your training partner wear a mouthpiece and headgear. But don't try to hit him in the head with your strike. Have him hold a focus mitt about eight to 10 inches away from his head. Then you'll be covered if you hit the mitt and drive it into his face or if you accidentally him."

A heavy bag can be used for developing power and speed to amplify the effectiveness of your spinning technique, Carter says. "But to get used to the timing, the slipping and moving, and the changing levels, you have to get in the ring and spar. Just be sure to do it safely."

After investing many hours in the dojo, you will be able to integrate all three spinning techniques into your fighting style, Carter insists. "Once you know how to execute them, adjust them to match your body," he says. "Find out what works for you."

In Shonie Carter's Own Words

• "The biggest thing to remember when you're throwing a spinning technique is to look over your shoulder and use your shoulder to protect your chin. Then, if your opponent punches, it'll graze your ear. That may hurt, but I'd rather my ear get grazed than get my jaw broken."

• "Little women will come to me and ask, 'What can I do against a 200-pound guy?' I say: 'Look, you shouldn't be in that situation, but if you must, even though you're so petite with those skinny little arms, you can inflict a lot of damage using your elbows. If a guy grabs you by the head, you can come around the top and pop! If he has you in a bear hug, he'll drop if you hit him clean—think temple, eye, bridge of nose and cheekbone."

• "For every action, there's an equal and opposite reaction; and for every move, there's an equal and opposite counter. And for that counter, there's an equal and opposite counter to that, and so on. While I was a wrestler in high school, my father told me once, 'Shonie, in a single game of chess there are more potential moves than there are stars in the sky.' I looked at him and said, 'Dad, in a single wrestling match, there are more moves potentially than there are in a game of chess.' He looked at me and said, 'Are you being funny?' And I said, 'No.' "

• "If you're throwing a spinning elbow technique in a sparring session, be careful because it's hard to slow it down. There have been times where I've let it rip. I hit a buddy of mine and chipped his tooth. I was like, 'Oops … sorry.' "

• "The heavy bag I use for power and speed because there's not a heavy bag in the world that's lost a boxing match. You can go 40 or 50 rounds, and that bag will still be sitting there swinging."

• "He dropped his hands and stepped in with a roundhouse, and my forearm caught him right in the throat. He went down. It didn't make that smack; it made a thud. I looked at him as he got up, and he's like, 'That hurt.' And the funny thing is that he shook my hand, and I hugged him and kissed him on the cheek. I said, 'Good fight, man, nice try.' He shook my hand three times in the ring and two more times outside after we got dressed. Then he came up to me and said, 'Shonie, I'm sorry for being a bad boy. I didn't mean to not shake your hand.' And I'm like, 'Trust me, you did.' And he said, 'No, I didn't mean to storm out of the ring and not shake your hand.' And I was like, 'It's OK. I have no hard feelings. You and I are still cool. Why don't I buy you a drink and an aspirin?' "

- "I'm a real weird animal. I fight from the southpaw leg. I tend to do weird stuff, which is why people don't expect me to win the fights that I do. I'm not a traditional, fundamental fighter."

- "He was talking about how good Matt Serra was. But I'm like, 'That's great, but if you put Matt Serra and me in a Greco-Roman match, I'd spank him 10 out of 10 times. If you put us in a freestyle match, I'd spank him 11 out of 11 times. But in sport *jujutsu,* he might beat me 9 out of 10 times.' "

- "In all spinning techniques, the idea is to keep yourself centered. Your arms aren't supposed to be flailing around like some drunk chicken."

- "Fighting is mental. I mean, there's a degree of physical, but hell, how many people have I defeated that were technically superior to me?"

- "I know for a fact that Dan Henderson has made more in 11 fights than I've made in my entire fighting career, and he's not 11-0. I got to get some Imodium AD."

- "The more money you pay, the better the show gets. You will get ring girls and people jumping and doing back flips. I will come out in a thong if you want. I will come in rappelling out of the rafters. They ain't got to pay me $31 million to box. Pay me half a million dollars, and I'll fight everyone on the fight card from bantamweight to heavyweight and make them look silly. I'll get some pectoral implants; I'll try to grow some, but I probably ain't growing much."

SECRETS OF THE HOOK
Does Power Prevail, or Is Precision Paramount?
by Evan Pantazi • Photos by Evan Pantazi • March 2003

You're watching a professional boxing match. In the middle of round two, you catch a glimpse of the champ's left hook, which drops the contender like a sack of potatoes. It looked like the punch barely touched him, but he's out cold, KO'd by a single blow. You begin musing: Wouldn't it be nice if my punch had that kind of guaranteed effectiveness? Wouldn't it be great if I could add that knockout blow to my self-defense arsenal?

Well, there is a concrete reason why some punches land with enough power to stop an elephant. It is the same reason why, unfortunately, most do not. This article will examine the issue, specifically with respect to the hook, so you will have a better grasp of the secrets to generating knockout power with your punch.

Primary Target

The head is the primary target for the hook punch because it is vulnerable and accessible. There are several areas on the head which, if struck at the correct angle, will render the opponent unconscious or at least cause him to collapse because of a loss of motor control. The reason more hook-punch knockouts are not seen in the ring has nothing to do with the

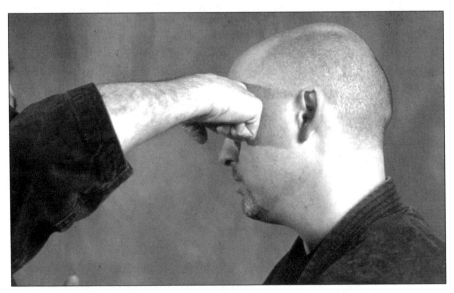

The group of pressure points located just to the outside of the eye socket must be struck downward and inward at a 45-degree angle.

 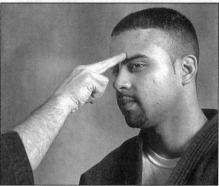

When an experienced fighter tucks his chin to his chest, the cluster of pressure points on the bridge of his nose can easily be accessed.

use of padded boxing gloves; rather, it stems from the angle at which the concussive force is delivered.

Most punches land at a 90-degree angle to the side of the head, and unfortunately for the puncher, no pressure points respond to that type of blow. The correct angle for the strike is 45 degrees. When a rising or dropping motion is used in conjunction with the proper angle, several targets on the head can be attacked. Interestingly, a few additional targets can be accessed when an attack is delivered at a 45-degree angle from the back of the head toward the front, but they are considered illegal in boxing.

Because the human body does not handle a 45-degree blow as well as it does a straight punch or a perpendicular strike, a precision hook punch can enable you to accomplish your goal of incapacitating your opponent without the use of massive amounts of power. Thus delivered, the hook becomes a tactical weapon for practitioners of all ring arts, including boxing, kickboxing and no-holds-barred fighting.

Proper Angles

If you execute a hook at an incorrect angle, you attack your opponent's bone and muscles using only your power. However, if you execute it at the correct angle, you attack his nervous system and your strike will have an amplified effect. There are two main categories into which the angled punch can be separated: the dropping hook and the rising hook. The dropping hook can be used to attack more targets, but the rising hook can be just as effective and often works well even with a boxing glove wrapped around your fist.

When you punch down and in toward the center of the neck with a

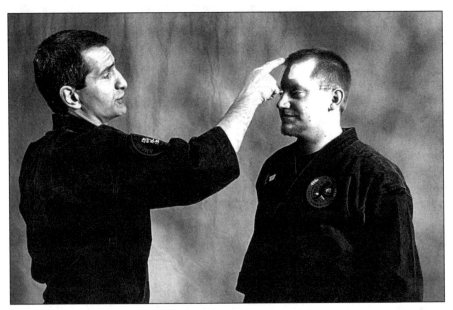

A group of vulnerable pressure points at the top of the forehead near the hairline can be targeted with a hook punch.

hooking action, you can target the focal point of nerves that lies directly between the chin and the hinge of the jaw (the point on the facial nerve where the buccal branch crosses). Your blow will cause a loss of motor control or unconsciousness.

Another effective target, the mental nerve, is positioned directly under the corner of the mouth on both sides of the chin. Once again, it must be struck down and in at a 45-degree angle toward the center of the neck. Your attack will have the same effect as a strike to the aforementioned target, but with additional shock to the brain stem. Consequently, the results will be even more dramatic.

Key Component

Grasping the concept of "polarity" is essential if you want to be an effective hook-puncher. Knowledge of it can make all your shots work better and with greater consistency—and that's a wonderful asset to have when the other guy is aiming to hurt you.

Human beings are bioelectrical creatures. Our bodies have a natural energy pattern when they function correctly, and disrupting that pattern can induce a loss of motor control or unconsciousness. The key components of polarity are *yin* and *yang,* or in Western terms, negative and positive. Once you know which strikes and stances are positive and which are negative, and how each affects various parts of the opponent's body, you will be able to short-circuit him. For example, if you elect to use a left hook to blast the right side of his head, you should lift the heel of your left foot for maximum effectiveness. The technique can work without your heel being raised, but it will be significantly more potent if it's off the ground.

Best Moves

Two single points and six clustered points are legal strike zones in the boxing and NHB ring. Therefore, no matter which way your opponent's head is positioned, you are guaranteed an open target for your hook punch.

If his head is up, a downward 45-degree hook can access either single point on the side of his jaw. Or it can travel downward and inward to strike the three-point cluster on the front of his jaw. Remember that these blows must be aimed in toward the center of the neck.

If your opponent has tucked his jaw in close to his shoulder—which most experienced fighters will do—the clusters of points on his forehead, on the side of his eye socket, in front of his ear and on the bridge of his nose will be your easiest targets. The points on the forehead and bridge of the nose must be struck down and in at a 45-degree angle toward the center of the skull to cause a loss of motor control or unconsciousness.

For the clusters on the side of his head, you must vary the angle slightly. The downward 45-degree hook is still used, but for the eyebrow cluster, you need to strike down and in toward the eyeball itself. For the cluster of points in front of the ear, once again you must strike down and in at a 45-degree angle, but this time it should be directed toward the center of the skull.

Two pressure points reside on each side of the face: One is near the chin (left) and one is in the middle of the jaw (right).

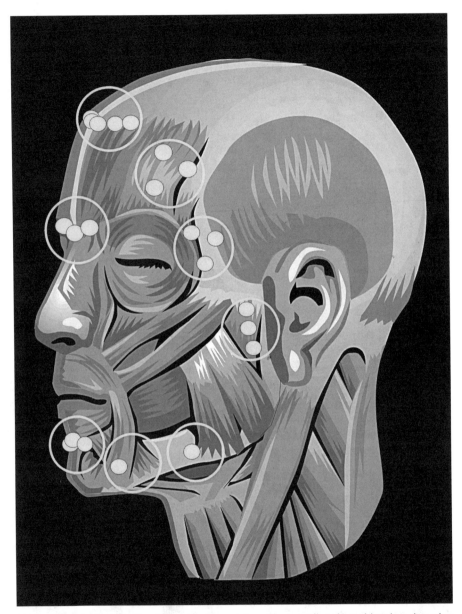

Although many beginners believe the hook is always delivered horizontally in front of their face, the author insists it is a versatile technique that can easily reach a variety of targets on the opponent's head.

No Trace

In self-defense, Westerners tend to fight with their fists, but Asian martial arts masters teach that the palm is often superior. A conventional punch delivered in a street fight may leave your hand broken and your adversary's head bruised and bleeding. More important, it may provide evidence of physical injury that can be used against you in a court of law.

It is preferable to defend yourself with a palm strike that uses the same hooking motion described above. It will minimize the risk of damaging your knuckles, and it will leave no marks for a lawyer to capitalize on. The only course correction you need to make before launching the open-hand attack involves keeping your foot flat on the floor. The reasoning behind the change is as follows: When you use the other side of your hand—the palm instead of the fist—you are taking advantage of the opposite electrical charge. When the heel on the side of your body you're using to strike is down, it is grounded. Therefore, it changes the electrical charge in that hand.

All this versatility makes *kyusho jitsu*, the art of pressure-point fighting, the ultimate martial skill. It can be used effectively in boxing, kickboxing and NHB fighting—and has in fact been seen in many fights. With slight modification, it can be used to drop an attacker on the street, and it does not require superhuman amounts of strength. Best of all, its techniques inflict little or no visible damage on the aggressor, leaving you with a much more arguable defense.

Conservation of Energy

Attacking the nervous system of your opponent with a precisely aimed hook punch is better than attacking his musculoskeletal structure with a power shot for several reasons:

- You will reap greater results.
- You will expend less energy.
- You will need less explosive power in your strike.
- You will experience less fatigue if you are forced to attempt the punch several times.
- You will remain more mobile because you will retain more of your energy.

—*E.P.*

POWER OF THE PUNCH

by Robert McLain • Photo by Sara Fogan • May 2003

Often in martial arts classes, we are told that some techniques are stronger or weaker than others. We strike the air and then a heavy bag to judge the power of our blows. Our knuckles redden, and we see the bag sway from the impact. But we don't know how strong our punches really are.

Out of curiosity, I decided to conduct several experiments to see how much of a "knockback" effect a 120-pound person would experience when punched by a 180-pound martial artist and compare it with the effect of a .45-caliber bullet. I was teaching in the kinesiology department at the University of Texas, Arlington, and running a martial arts school at the time, so I took advantage of the available resources.

I used the standard equations for determining kinetic energy and linear momentum to calculate the strength of three kinds of strikes—the straight punch, the reverse punch and the skip reverse punch—as well as the afore-mentioned bullet fired from a Ruger P90 handgun. For help with the ballistic component of the experiment, I turned to Ron Fazio, a forensics-firearms examiner for the Fort Worth Police Department crime laboratory.

Because I planned to do the punching, we went to the Tarrant County Medical Examiner's Office, where the weight (mass) of my arm, legs, head and torso was measured. Next, we constructed a ballistic pendulum, which is the standard device used to demonstrate the conservation of momentum and calculate how much energy is transferred from a moving object into a stationary body. We also acquired a radar gun—the same equipment baseball clubs use to measure the velocity of pitches—to gauge the speed of my punches. Darcia Meador, the rangemaster for the Fort Worth Police Department, helped us use an electronic chronograph to measure the speed of the bullets.

We found that a 230-grain high-velocity, hollow-point bullet had an average speed of 932 feet per second or 635 miles per hour. If completely stopped by an attacker's 120-pound body, it would cause him to be knocked backward at a rate of .25 feet per second.

When we used the pendulum to test the martial arts moves, we found that a straight punch executed from a horse stance would knock back the opponent at a rate of two feet per second, or eight times as fast as the bullet. The reverse punch thrown from a back stance also had a knock-back rate of two feet per second. A skip reverse punch—which is executed the same way as the reverse punch except that the striker skips forward while performing the technique—knocked the opponent backward at three feet per second. That's a whopping 12 times faster than the handgun.

Those results may surprise you. After all, bullets are much more lethal than punches, but it would seem that punches possess more power. While strikes are significantly slower and do not penetrate the skin, they will push the object being impacted, which accounts for their greater ability to displace a target. So the next time you see someone in a movie get thrown backward or fly through the air after being shot by a handgun, you can chuckle and think, "That gun can't do that, but I can."

The author's research shows that punches transfer significantly more power to a target than bullets do. (For illustrative purposes, *taekwondo* expert Philip Ameris is shown punching.)

THE REALITY-BASED PUNCH

by Jim Wagner • Photo by Rick Hustead • January 2004

The doctrine of reality-based fighting holds that to make your closed-fist strikes as effective as they can be, you must consider the following three principles:

Technique Train: It refers to the step-by-step order in which each component of the punch happens. It starts with the conflict position. Your weight should be distributed equally on your feet, with your body bladed and your arms up. Your lead hand should be on your centerline just below your chin, and your rear hand should float around your cheek. (The term "conflict position" is used in place of "fighting stance" because "fighting" indicates premeditation toward physical contact, whereas "conflict" does not necessarily indicate a physical altercation. You should remain cognizant of the words you use during a conflict because you'll inevitably face law-enforcement officials and the judicial system if you use your martial arts skills for self-defense.)

The next component is hand position. Tightly close your fist by curling your fingers and placing your thumb over your index and middle digits. The striking points—the knuckles of your first and second fingers—should be aligned with the bones of your forearm.

Third is the line of trajectory. Your fist should travel along a straight path from where it's launched to where it hits the target.

The final component is the recovery phase. After your fist makes contact, your arm is retracted and cocked again in case a follow-up technique is needed.

Stopping Power: In the world of firearms, the bigger a bullet is and the more powder it has to propel it, the greater its stopping power. It's the same for arm strikes. The goal in any conflict is to stop the aggressor, not to kill or injure him. When you're on the witness stand, you should say, "I struck him to stop him, and I stopped when he stopped aggressing me." And it's better to stop him with one or two good strikes than to allow him to continue assaulting you while you execute 10 rapid-fire techniques.

To boost your stopping power, remember the "piston concept." It teaches that your punch should trace a straight line to its target, then retrace that path to its starting position—just like a piston in an engine. Whether the strike is horizontal (such as a hook punch) or vertical (such as an uppercut), this concept simplifies the motion and emphasizes the power stroke.

Target Acquisition: The target you select depends on the level of force you plan to use. If you're just trying to control an unruly brother-in-law, you will probably aim for different targets than you would if you were fighting back against a terrorist on a plane. As such, it's useful to separate the body into areas (from most to least injurious): The red zone includes the head, neck, spine, kidneys and groin; the orange zone includes the torso and pelvic area; and the yellow zone is the limbs.

Striking the surface of a target does you little good. Your goal should be to penetrate it. Instead of trying to just hit the aggressor's rib cage, vow to drive your fist into his lungs.

Training Tips: It's unsafe to use full power while sparring with a human being, so you must limit your punches to 75 percent of your maximum. To develop stopping power and hone your target-acquisition ability, imagine a conflict scenario and strike a heavy bag as if it were a violent opponent. Go full-bore for about 15 seconds, which is about as long as a real conflict will last. Then simulate taking your adversary down and making a citizen's arrest or escaping. Whatever you do, don't just stand there. Condition yourself not just for the striking portion of a fight but for the complete conflict.

Reality-based punching makes use of the "piston concept," whereby your fist plows straight into its target, then reverses course and returns to its starting position.

237

PUNCHES VS. PALM STRIKES

by Kathy Long • January 2005

A *Black Belt* reader recently asked me to describe the advantages and disadvantages of using a punch vs. a palm strike. The rule of thumb is, the target you're aiming at and the nature of the conflict you're involved in will generally determine which technique you should employ.

Whenever you punch somebody with your fist, you risk injuring your hand. The blow may knock out your adversary or send him sprawling to the floor. However, if the strike impacts a bony part of his body—such as his head—you can break the bones in your hand.

Wrapping your hands like a professional boxer and wearing boxing gloves or bag gloves will preserve the integrity of your bones to some extent in the ring, but neither option is practical on the street. Besides, neither will prevent injury 100 percent of the time. Remember that your hands are designed to accomplish delicate tasks, not to punch an opponent's lights out.

Conventional punches use the knuckles as the primary striking surface, and for many martial artists that's a good reason not to use them to hit an opponent in the head. Other strikes utilize nearby parts of the hand, however, and some are better and some are worse.

For example, the ridgehand uses the side of the first knuckle of the index finger. The nature of your training and whether you include body-hardening exercises will determine whether you should consider slamming that technique into someone's skull.

The hammerfist employs the edge of the hand near the pinkie. It can be used to inflict quite a bit of damage to someone's face, back of the head or skull with minimal risk of injury.

A punch is better suited to striking an assailant in the midsection because driving a fist into soft tissue creates a sharper pain.

A caveat: It takes considerable practice to be able to hit any target accurately. That's particularly true when you're going for a smaller target such as the groin because when you're being attacked and you're scared half out of your mind, your adrenaline will be pumping, you'll develop tunnel vision and you'll be unable to remember what you need to do. If the aforementioned hand techniques aren't already ingrained in your muscle memory, you're probably not going to be able to use them effectively when you need to.

Fortunately, striking with the heel of the palm gives you a little more margin for error because it employs a larger surface area. And you can throw a palm-heel strike harder than you can throw a punch because you won't be afraid of breaking your hand. I often have my students throw a palm heel as hard as possible against a concrete wall. However, when I ask them to make a fist and punch the same wall using the same amount of strength, they look at me like I'm crazy. They all know that no matter how tight they form their fist, smacking it into a hard surface means there's a good chance of breaking a bone.

The palm is also perfect for hitting the head because it can be thrown with the same velocity as a punch and can therefore deliver the same energy. You can hit someone hard enough to fracture the occipital bone or cheekbone, which will leave him with a black eye and probably a concussion. Then, if need be, you can use your fingers to gouge his eyes.

If your life is in danger, another obvious target for the palm strike is the groin. The technique is ideal because you have a much greater chance of striking the testicles and inflicting debilitating pain. (By the way, if you ever need to increase that pain, follow up your strike by grabbing and squeezing the goods.)

For serious self-defense purposes, consider effecting a palm strike to the ear. It can rupture an eardrum and end the fight in a fraction of a second. The pain is excruciating, and the ringing sensation often blocks all other sounds. A fringe benefit for the defender is that the technique also disrupts the attacker's equilibrium, possibly leaving him nauseous and unable to stand.

This discussion underscores an often-overlooked facet of martial arts training: learning about human anatomy. Such knowledge will help you understand which parts of the body are more vulnerable to certain strikes and which natural weapons are best for striking them. The increased awareness that results will boost the effectiveness of all your techniques while reducing your risk of being hurt.

COMBAT SLAP
It's Not Your Mother's Self-Defense Technique!
by Jeff Menapace • Photos by Jeff Menapace • January 2005

"I have never had anyone stay on their feet after I delivered a slap."

So says Dave Briggs, a United Kingdom-based self-defense legend and the survivor of hundreds of violent encounters during the 11 years he worked as a doorman.

If you think Briggs' use of the word "slap" is a humorous description of a good punch or maybe even a slang term for a barrage of techniques he used to overwhelm an attacker, you're on the wrong track. He's talking about an actual slap delivered to the side of an assailant's head. Of course, it's not an ordinary slap like you'd see on *As the World Turns*. No, this baby is a different beast altogether.

Punching vs. Slapping

The first hand technique most martial artists learn is the punch—and for good reason. When properly honed, it can be an efficient instrument for transmitting awesome power to a target. As any practitioner of the combat arts will attest, one good punch to the jaw can determine the outcome of a fight—usually by marking the beginning of nap time for the recipient.

So if a punch to the jaw is so effective, why bother with a slap? Consider the human head for a moment. Because most people need their brains to function properly, their gray matter needs some solid protection. Enter the human skull. It's that hard, bony structure that also happens to contain a bunch of sharp teeth that can carry all sorts of nasty germs capable of doing a whole lot of damage should they find a way into your skin.

The skull is there for one reason: To protect the brain. If you decide to smash your comparatively small and unprotected fists into someone's skull—or even worse, to drive them into his teeth—something's got to give, and it'll probably be your metacarpals.

But wait: We were talking about punching the jaw, not the skull. And the beauty of striking the jaw is that it gives when hit, thus sparing your hand. And when you're terrified, with adrenaline pouring through your veins, you can hit the jaw every time with spot-on accuracy, right?

Wrong. Accuracy is one of the first things to go out the window when you're feeling the effects of adrenaline. Briggs has suffered hand damage on numerous occasions because he used his fists to strike an aggressor's head. He says it's not uncommon for a hand to blow up to twice its normal

When confronted by an assailant, Jeff Menapace (left) raises his hands in a nonthreatening manner (1). As the man becomes more aggressive, Menapace drops his right hand until it's out of the opponent's line of vision (2). The martial artist then catches the assailant off-guard with a pre-emptive slap to the face (3).

size after a misplaced punch. (Even when you punch correctly, the fact that you're smashing bone into bone means there will be some damage to your own hands.)

241

 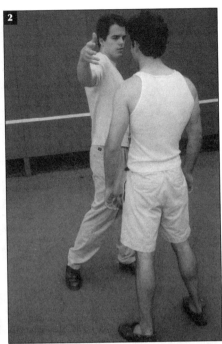

MECHANICS OF THE COMBAT SLAP: Jeff Menapace (left) relaxes his striking arm as he begins whipping his hip to create momentum in his upper body (1). His open hand then travels up and across, minimizing the chance the opponent will detect it (2).

How It Works

This is where the slap shines. Not only is the chance of injuring your hand negligible, but the target for the technique is the entire side of your opponent's head. That means you can hit his ear, cheek, neck or jaw. Pinpoint accuracy isn't necessary.

Wondering what effect a slap will have? Briggs has used the technique as a pre-emptive strike on more than 100 people, and he claims 80 percent of those encounters were knockouts. The other 20 percent of the time, his opponents were incapacitated to the point at which he could easily escape or deliver a follow-up blow.

It's obvious that the slap can be just as effective as a punch to the jaw. Curiously, the mechanisms by which the two strikes achieve a knockout are different. A heavy punch to the jaw causes an immediate shaking of the brain, which produces a temporary blackout and results in a KO. The goal of a slap, however, is to overload the central nervous system with more information than it can process, thus producing a knockout-like effect.

When you strike someone with a small surface such as the front of your

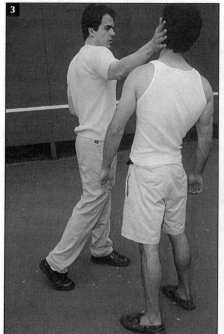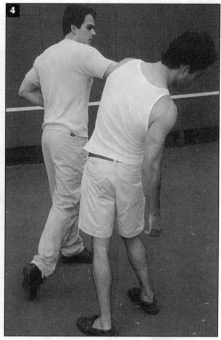

He makes contact with the man's head (3) and continues his motion past the target (4).

knuckles but miss the bull's-eye, your opponent's brain recognizes that it's been struck and deals with the pain. Then it tells his body to continue fighting. However, when you deliver a slap to the side of his face using the entire flat of your hand, you provide his central nervous system with more information than it can handle. That causes his brain to shut down.

Relaxation and the Double-Hip

The only way to transfer sufficient energy to such a large area is through relaxation. Briggs identifies it as the most important component of the slap. When relaxed, your body is capable of imparting a tremendous amount of energy to a target, and the double-hip principle provides the perfect delivery mechanism.

Briggs learned the intricacies of the slap and the double-hip movement from Peter Consterdine, a well-known British author who serves as a chief instructor for the British Combat Association. Consterdine has polished his slapping technique to such an extent that when he practices it, his opponents can feel the energy passing through several inches of foam padding and into their body.

The assailant (right) approaches and immediately invades the defender's space, forcing the defender to raise his hands for protection (1). As the tension increases, the defender lowers his striking hand and prepares to grab his opponent's lead arm (2). The defender immobilizes the limb and propels a combat slap into the man's face (3).

The goal of the double-hip technique is to provide a door-hinge-like effect, which is a whipping action similar to the way you serve a tennis ball. The hip on your nonstriking side is the first to move. It creates the door hinge and is followed by the other hip. That provides a recoil and whiplash effect in your upper body, accelerating the weapon. This twin motion of the hips is the source of the principle's moniker. Compare it to the standard karate or boxing method in which the hand and hip move together, and you'll notice a huge difference in the amount of energy generated.

Visualization

A key element in developing the double-hip principle and making your slap more efficient is visualization. Briggs says you should envision your hand weighing 20 pounds. That forces you to employ your hips to whip the strike into the target.

When you first try the combat slap, you'll probably encounter a few obstacles. If you simply snap the blow out using your arm and shoulder muscles, it will wind up being similar to a quick hook punch delivered with an open hand—and that's not what you want.

Another common mistake involves treating the move like it's a circular palm-heel strike. It's not. The technique is a slap, and you want your hand to have as little tension as possible for maximum energy transfer.

By pretending it's a heavy weight dangling at your side, you'll be able to completely relax your arm, and your hips will become the only means available to swing it.

Once you grasp the concept of the heavy hand, you should visualize your strike traveling *through* the target. It's almost a cliché in the martial arts world, but it's very true. Don't simply slap the target; slap through it so forcefully that your energy transfer moves your body past where your target would have been.

Disguised Delivery

While the mechanics of the combat slap are crucial, the setup is equally important. You could have the most powerful handgun in the world, but if you're slow on the draw, you'll never get a chance to fire it before you're gunned down. Delivering the slap in a real-life encounter is no different. While Briggs admits that it's his preferred hand technique and that he has supreme confidence in it, he points out that it's useful mainly as a pre-emptive strike.

The mechanics and delivery of the blow mandate that you be stationary when you launch it. Therefore, it works best when used after you've attempted to verbally defuse a hostile situation and failed, because that's when you should strike first.

The secret to succeeding with the slap revolves around initiating it before your opponent detects it. Because it's not a quick-twitch movement, by nature it will always be a little slower, but that can be remedied by disguising your delivery. Remember that it's the punch you don't see that knocks you out.

The optimal setup starts with simple dialogue, body language and gesturing. Briggs advises standing with your arms out to your sides in what Geoff Thompson refers to as the "exclamation fence." You'll look as if you're not a threat and are trying to reason with the aggressor. In reality, your striking hand is out of the attacker's line of vision, and your nonstriking hand is making big sweeping gestures directly in front of his eyes. Because the majority of people suffer from tunnel vision when their adrenaline is pumping, he'll probably focus solely on your nonstriking hand. Then, when you spring into action, you'll take him by surprise.

Confidence in Technique

To become proficient at the slap, you must first witness it being performed by a competent instructor, then repeat it countless times until it feels right. Because the principle of the technique contradicts the way most martial artists interpret the mechanics that are involved, it's easy to develop a "physical delivery" instead of a relaxed one.

A good way to practice and get feedback is to have your partner hold the pads while you strike. Ask him to provide input regarding how well you disguise and deliver the blow. When you need to work on generating power, try a heavy bag.

It's essential to develop confidence in your technique, Briggs says, because you're unlikely to fire an effective strike if you're hesitant or unsure. When he was ready to make the jump from punching to slapping, Briggs says he just did it. He'd been practicing so diligently that he knew it wouldn't fail. When the moment of truth came, he executed it without hesitation—and it produced an easy knockout.

Although the mere mention of using a slap as a self-defense technique can elicit snickers from experts and novices alike, it would be foolhardy to overlook it. After all, when two street-savvy martial artists like Dave Briggs and Peter Consterdine claim a success rate of 100 percent with it, it behooves you to take a second look.

Legal Defense

Dave Briggs loves to tell his students a story about an incident in which he used the combat slap on an assailant who was accompanied by six other men. The technique proved so effective that it knocked out the aggressor and caused him to fall into his accomplices, producing a picture-perfect domino effect.

When the man regained consciousness, he immediately blamed his friends for having hit him. Briggs' disguised delivery had been that good. The man grew even more distraught when he learned that Briggs had laid him out with a simple slap.

That brings up another potential benefit of using the slap as a pre-emptive strike: In the eyes of the law, it looks and sounds anything but vicious. And the victim might be so embarrassed about having been KO'd by a slap that he elects not to contact the authorities about it.

—J.M.

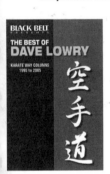

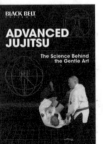